OLD WEST MERCHANTS

True Tales of the Old West

by

Charles L. Convis

Watercolor Cover by Mary Anne Convis

PIONEER PRESS, Inc., CARSON CITY, NEVADA

Library of Congress Catalog Card Number: 96-68502

ISBN 1-892156-20-2

CONTENTS

BORN FOR THE FUR TRADE   (Antione and Louis Robidoux)   2
THE BROTHERS BENT   (Charles and William Bent)   4
NAMES ON THE LAND   (Bob Dempsey)   11
BEEF KING OF MONTANA   (Conrad Kohrs)   12
LONELY FERRYWOMAN   (Emma Batchelor Lee French)   18
MERCHANT OF AMPLE MEANS   (Ledyard Frink)   21
THE GREAT CONDENSER   (Gail Borden)   24
DOAN'S CROSSING   (Jonathan and Calvin Doan)   29
JACKASS MAIL PIONEERS   (George Chorpenning and
                                    Absalom Woodward   32
BETTER THAN SHOVELS AND WHEELBARROWS (David Staples)   34
WHEELBARROW JOHNNY   (John Studebaker)   36
GOLD RUSH TRADER   (John Sloane Collins)   38
RED, WHITE, AND BROTHERHOOD   (Jesse Chisholm)   40
THE HERCULES OF EXPRESSMEN   (Dave Butterfield)   42
CHATTEL MORTGAGE   (Grant Marsh and Nelson Miles)   44
TEN YEARS IN NEVADA   (Mary McNair Mathews)   46
BUSINESS SECRET AT ADOBE WALLS   (Wright and John Mooar)   48
GREAT MEN THINK ALIKE   (Hiram Sibley, Ezra Cornell, and
                                    Edward Creighton)   52
NORTHERN EXPANSION   (Perry McDonough Collins)   54
THE MAN WITH A THOUSAND PARTNERS   (J. C. Penney, Jr.)   60

ORDERING INFORMATION   62

ILLUSTRATIONS

CHARLES BENT   6
CONRAD KOHRS   14
AUGUSTA KRUSE KOHRS   15
GAIL BORDEN   25
PROPOSED TRANSPACIFIC TELEGRAPH LINE   55
TELEGRAPH CONSTRUCTION IN BRITISH COLUMBIA   57

BORN FOR THE FUR TRADE

Antione and Louis Robidoux were born for the fur trade. Their great grandfather, Andre Robidoux, migrated from France to Quebec in 1667. Their father, Joseph Robidoux II, moved from Quebec to St. Louis in 1770, where he married and had ten children. Antione and Louis were the seventh and eighth children in the family.

When Joseph II died, older brother Joseph III became leader of the family. He founded St. Joseph, Missouri, named for his patron saint, and he encouraged his brothers to develop the fur trade at interior posts west of Missouri. Antoine and Louis went the farthest, eight hundred miles to Santa Fe.

They arrived in 1824, just three years after Mexico had gained its independence from Spain. They made connections with an old friend and ally, Auguste Chouteau, and Antoine spent the next two or three years trapping and trading in the unexplored wilderness to the northwest. Beaver were plentiful, the powerful fur companies headquartered in St. Louis had not moved in, and the friendly Ute Indians welcomed trade for American goods.

Louis apparently spent most of his time on the road trading between St. Louis, Santa Fe, El Paso, and Chihuahua. In 1825 he brought brothers François and Michael back to Santa Fe with him.

It was also a good time to be handsome young men, gifted with social graces, and fluent in the Spanish language. Santa Fe society welcomed Antoine and Louis. In 1825 the citizens elected Antione to the Santa Fe City Council. In 1828 he married Carmel Benevides, the governor's adopted daughter. About the same time, Louis married Guadalupe Garcia. Both brothers became naturalized Mexican citizens in 1829. The next year Antoine became president of the Santa Fe City Council.

In 1834 Louis followed Antoine to the Santa Fe City Council. Five years later he became president, the same office his brother had once held. Both brothers earned reputations for fairness in their service as alcaldes, where they adjudicated local disputes. New Orleans reporter Matt Field, wrote that Louis Robidoux "shares the rule over the people almost equally with the governor and the priests."

Antoine's fame in history rests on his building two trading forts in the intermontane corridor running northwest from Santa Fe. He built the first, usually called Fort Uncompahgre, on the Gunnison River a short distance below the mouth of the Uncompahgre River in present western Colorado. The exact location was obliterated by ranchers in the 1880s, but the fort has been reconstructed in the outskirts of Delta. Through this fort the Indians of wsetern Colorado, Utah, southern Idaho, and southwestern Wyoming had their first contact with European civilization.

Antoine built a second fort, Fort Uintah, near the mouth of White Rocks Creek on the Uintah River in present northeastern Utah. Louis took charge of Fort Uncompahgre while Antoine built the other fort.

In 1842 Marcus Whitman and Amos L. Lovejoy became the first white men to travel the intermontane corridor from Fort Hall on the Snake River toward Santa Fe. They rode through both Fort Uintah—where they met Antoine—and Fort Uncompahgre on their famous winter ride.

The brothers operated a tannery and a grist mill in Santa Fe. By 1844 Louis was also operating an ironworks in that city. In that year he moved to California, leaving Guadalupe and the children behind. He bought two leagues of land (about nine thousand acres) in the area of present Riverside. Soon after, he bought the Rancho San Jacinto in the same area. He returned to Santa Fe to bring Guadalupe and the children out. A young son died on the journey. By 1846 he had a grist mill, one of the first in southern California. Louis never returned to Santa Fe or Missouri.

In late 1844 Antoine abandoned Fort Uncompahgre and settled in St. Joseph, Missouri. Two years later he interpreted for General Stephen Watts Kearny on his campaign to the West in the War Against Mexico. In December, 1846, he was severely wounded by a lance-wielding Californian in the Battle of San Pasqual. He returned to St. Joseph, where he and Carmel adopted a young daughter.

Antoine's significance in Southwest history was indicated in 1853 when John Gunnison made the first survey through central Colorado. He crossed what was later called Mosca Pass in Alamosa County and called it Robideau's Pass in his journal. (The pass is apparently near what is now called Blanca Pass on highway maps.) The name makes one wonder if Antoine, in making his rides from Fort Uncompahgre to Missouri, rode up the Gunnison—of course, it wasn't called that then—and crossing Cotechopa Pass and the San Luis Valley. This route would have been more direct than dropping down through Santa Fe. John C. Fremont, "The Great Explorer" also used Robideau Pass in 1848.

Antoine died in modest circumstances in 1860 in St. Joseph. Louis died a wealthy man in California eight years later. The brothers contributed significantly to the early development of the southwest fur trade.

Suggested reading: William S. Wallace, "Antoine Robidoux" in LeRoy Hafen (ed.) *Mountain Men and the Fur Trade, v. 4* (Glendale: Arthur H. Clark Co., 1966).

THE BROTHERS BENT

When Lewis and Clark reached St. Louis on their return from the Pacific, a six-year-old boy, small for his age, watched the excitement intently. The Silas Bent family had arrived from the east less than a week before, and Charles, oldest of the four children, thrilled to the talk of the three-year expedition just ending. He knew that his grandfather had helped pitch tea into Boston Harbor and had then joined the Minutemen after the skirmish at Lexington. He may have wondered if his life would be affected by the talk of these buckskin-clad soldiers about tall mountains, shining rivers, and strange Indians in the mysterious land to the west. The family would eventually grow to eleven children, but William, ten years younger, was always Charles' favorite.

Silas had come west as a surveyor, and was later appointed by President Madison to the Territorial Supreme Court. His sons went to good schools, but not for very long; the excitement in the west was too much to ignore. We don't know when Charles found work with Manuel Lisa's Missouri Fur Company, but by 1824, when he was twenty-five, he was well established with them.

Until then, all probes to the rich beaver country in the mountains went up the Missouri River. But Indian resistance and competing companies made some men try an overland route. In September 1827, forty-five men and a hundred horses loaded with trade goods headed up the Platte. They included Charles Bent and the other four partners of the re-organized Missouri Fur Company, as well as eighteen-year-old William.

Blizzards and horse-stealing Crow Indians forced the men to bury their trade goods and flee through deep snows to the ice-cold valley of the Green River in present Wyoming. There they wintered with another group that had come up from Taos. It was originally led by Sylvestre Pratte, and its two dozen men included Old Bill Williams, Tom Smith, and Milton Sublette.

The men from Taos had been trying to reach the fur country of the Southwest. Colorado was particularly attractive with its four huge, mountain-rimmed bowls. In the most northerly of these, Pratte had died and Smith had been wounded by Indians. Smith's name changed to Peg Leg when he amputated his own lower leg, with Sublette finishing the job after Smith passed out. The tough survivors had elected twenty-five-year-old Cerán St. Vrain their leader.

When winter ended, the Taos men returned there, and the Missouri Fur men returned to the Missouri. But their Wyoming cache had leaked, ruining the trade goods, and Charles and his partners learned on their return that the American Fur Company now controlled the Missouri River. In addition Charles learned that his father had died about the time they were struggling through the snow. Now he was the oldest man in the family.

In 1829 Charles and William went down the Santa Fe Trail to Taos in a wagon train which elected Charles captain. They renewed their friendship with St. Vrain, and made a new friend in Kit Carson, a few months younger than William. Eventually Carson would name two of his sons after Charles and William. "Equals to the Bent Brothers were never seen in the mountains," he often said.

Charles had a letter of introduction to the governor in Santa Fe, but a brave act by William the following winter had more significance for the brothers' future in the fur trade.

William went north with other independent trappers, and they made winter camp on the Arkansas River in present Colorado. A Cheyenne war party appeared, looking for Ute enemies. When they left, two of them stayed behind with the trappers. Then fierce Comanches rode up. They were enemies of all local tribes and a feared menace to all whites. William hid the Cheyennes among the trade goods, but the Comanches saw moccasin tracks and demanded to know where the Cheyennes were. William instantly and stubbornly insisted that all the warriors had left, and the Comanches backed down. The gratitude of the Cheyennes would have far-reaching consequences.

In 1830 Charles and St. Vrain continued as independents, trading between Independence and Santa Fe, and William trapped all the way to the Gila, where his party had to fight Indians. That December, Charles and St. Vrain formed their partnership. 1831 was the first boom year of the trade with a total of a half million dollars in goods moving west.

The next year, Charles' 18-year-old brother George and 16-year-old brother Robert traveled with him. Bent-St. Vrain began hauling trade goods north from Taos to the Arkansas to supply William's stockade at the mouth of Fountain Creek, where he had hidden the two Cheyennes before (near present Pueblo). That is when Charles realized that a large central fort, preferably of adobe to be safe against fire, would be necessary to hold the vast, unexploited area against competing traders.

On their way down the Arkansas toward home, the four brothers met a large party of Cheyennes who were delighted to see their friend again. When Charles explained in sign language his plans for a new fort, the Indians suggested that it be built twenty-five miles downriver from the mouth of the Purgatory at a favorite Cheyenne camping spot called Big Timbers. There would be shelter, abundant firewood and horse feed, and enough women to tan all the hides the traders could obtain. Charles knew the area was an uneasy border between Cheyennes, Arapahoes, and Kiowa-Apaches to the north, Utes to the west, and Comanches and Kiowas to the south. In

CHARLES BENT

Denver Public Library, Western History Collection

addition, wandering parties of Gros Ventres, Crows, and Shoshoni often came to visit or raid enemies. We don't know why Charles decided to build about a dozen miles upstream from the mouth of the Purgatory, but evidence suggests that he later regretted not following the Indians' advice.

The next year, 1833, Charles continued in charge of the supply trains and the trading while William and St. Vrain built the huge fort. No other fort between the Mississippi and the Pacific approached it in size. Rectangular, its 137-foot front wall was fourteen feet high and three feet or more thick. The 178-foot side walls were the same height and thickness. Eighteen-foot round towers rose at the southeast and northwest corners. Muskets and small cannons could sweep all walls with defensive fire. Sabers and lances hung inside the towers.

The 7-foot main gate was made from thick planks, sheathed in iron. The open plaza was surrounded on four sides by about twenty-five rooms. A second story was added as business grew. Eventually there was an owners' room with bar and billiard table. Corrals behind the fort had six-foot high walls with cacti planted on top to discourage scaling. No Indian attack could force the walls. A siege could starve the garrison out, but the owners gambled that Indians were too erratic in nature to maintain a siege.

Further north the fur companies were cutting each other's throats over a diminishing trade. Buffalo hides would now be most important, and Bent-St. Vrain were ready. Charles continued to look after the wagons rolling to Independence and back, and St. Vrain looked after the Taos end of the business, so William handled the trade out of the new fort. Buffalo hides were prime in winter, so their traders, working in groups of two or three, did most of their work then. They traded as far north as the Arikara and Sioux in Dakota. While the Bent-St. Vrain traders were considerably above their competition in business morality, they still used liquor to get business. Once, William hauled three cartloads of whiskey-filled kegs to a Cheyenne village on the North Platte.

Business grew, and in late 1835 or early 1836 Charles married Ignacia Jaramillo, a widow with a four-year-old daughter. She was about twenty and a beauty. She would bear Charles five children, two of whom died in infancy. From now on, Taos would remain his home.

William married Owl Woman, a Cheyenne, about 1837. Her father, Gray Thunder, was the holiest man in the Cheyenne nation, having custody of the four sacred medicine arrows.

By 1837 New Mexico simmered with unrest. Texas had won its independence the year before and even claimed the land to the Rio Grande, which included Taos and Santa Fe. When a governor was sent from Mexico to replace the native governor, the Pueblo Indians revolted. Manuel Armijo, who had been governor ten years before, secretly connived to encourage a revolution. The insurrectionists defeated the new governor's forces, beheaded the governor, and the Pueblos moved into the governor's palace. Then Armijo organized his own army and overthrew the insurrectionists he had secretly encouraged. He had their leaders killed and advised Mexico that he had put down the revolt. He was again made governor.

Meanwhile competition between the American Fur Company and Bent-St. Vrain continued. In 1838 they agreed to divide the west between them, the American Fur Company staying north of the Platte - North Platte, and Bent-St. Vrain staying south. Both companies prospered.

As part of the War against Mexico, Stephen Watts Kearny's Army of the West occupied Santa Fe on August 18, 1846. Governor Armijo fled, and the army appointed Charles Bent civil governor. The new officials, mostly merchants, had overwhelming problems administering a newly-conquered territory. Charles wrote Secretary of State James Buchanan for help, but it came slowly. The new government had no courts, no lawbooks, no translators, no mail service, and no way of raising taxes or paying for government officials, employees, or supplies.

Before the problems could be solved, the Pueblo Indians, still smoldering about their overthrow nine years before and reinforced this time by dissident New Mexicans, attacked. In the slaughter that followed, the insurgents shouted, "Kill the young ones, too. Don't let them grow up and trouble us again!" When the insurgents reached Charles' home, Ignacia brought his pistols. He shook his head sadly, realizing that violence on his part would lead to a massacre of women and children alike.

It was just after seven and growing light when Charles heard them scaling the walls. "What do you want?" he shouted. The entire household gathered around him in their nightclothes. A confused roar answered his question. He told Ignacia and the servants to dig through the adobe wall to the adjoining house, whose doorway might not be watched. "I'll stall for as much time as I can," he said quietly.

The women dug with a poker and large spoons in a back room while Charles offered money to his attackers. They hooted him down. Ten-year-old Alfredo came to his side. "Let's fight them papa," the boy said.

Charles gently pushed the boy back to his mother while calling through the door to suggest a council so that grievances could be aired. Blows sounded on the door, and he heard men tearing at the roof. He could not see how the women were doing. A gun butt broke a window. Still striving desperately for time, he offered to surrender if the mob would spare the other Americans in Taos.

A fusillade of musket fire splintered the door. A bullet struck his stomach. The door crashed in, and arrows struck his face, his chest. He staggered to the rear of the house. The women had made a hole and had pushed the children through. They reached for Charles and dragged him forward, but it was too late. An Indian grabbed him and threw him to the floor. Others yelled and, as Pueblos could, scalped him with a bowstring. Ignacia stayed behind, begging for the children's lives.

Some Indians continued mutilating Charles' body. Others yelled, "You fools, keep him alive as a hostage." The Pueblos milled about uncertainly. Then they told the women to stay in the house as prisoners. They tacked Charles' scalp to a board and went off, howling for fresh prey. All that day and the next, while Indians looted and burned the merchants' stores, the women and children waited beside Charles' body, lying in a pool of drying blood. Finally, friendly Mexicans came, took the body away and buried it secretly where the Indians could not find it. Others took the mourning family in. For them the revolution was over.

When the Cheyenne chiefs heard of Charles' murder, they wanted to lead their tribes against the insurgents. William Bent refused, saying it was a white man's problem. The army had created it; let the soldiers wage war if it became necessary. But when word came that rebel troops were advancing to help the insurgents, William and St. Vrain recruited a company of volunteers from the mountain men and merchants in Taos. Outnumbered 5 to 1, the army and volunteers defeated the insurgents.

With whites at war with Mexico, hostile tribes attacked throughout the southern plains. For fifteen years the Bent-St. Vrain Company had preached peace, but now there was no peace. Pawnees, Navajos, Comanches, and Kiowas killed forty-seven Americans that summer. The Comanches and Kiowas begged the Cheyennes to join in. Although their Arapaho allies showed some belligerence, the Cheyennes refused. William's courageous hiding of two warriors from certain death was still affecting history.

Later in 1847, Owl Woman died while bearing William their fourth child. When William held the baby he thought of his brother, brutally murdered shortly before. He named the baby Charles. Older boys had been named George and Robert after other uncles.

Under Cheyenne custom, the husband of an older sister could also take a younger sister for his wife if he wished. Yellow Woman was very close to older sister Owl Woman and had spent much time in the Bent tipi. Apparently William had never claimed his marital rights, but now with Owl Woman dead and a new baby to raise, he married Yellow Woman.

William and St. Vrain dissolved their partnership in 1849. That year cholera wiped out half of the Southern Cheyennes. A despondent William decided to abandon the fort built sixteen years before. He knew the army was interested in it. It had bought the American Fur Company fort in Wyoming and renamed it Fort Laramie. But he didn't ask for an offer. He hauled out twenty wagon loads of equipment and supplies and led the wagon train five miles away. He rode back alone, scattered kegs of gunpowder around, applied the torch, and rode out the gate. Behind, he heard the death explosion of the center of the greatest trading empire on the plains.

Then, to everyone's surprise, he moved downriver to the Big Timbers where the Cheyennes had originally told him he should build. There he built three log cabins connected together in a U shape, and began trading again.

Trade was good, buffalo were thick, and Indian women soon began approaching through the trees, carrying buffalo robes. Also, Yellow Woman bore their first child, his fifth.

In 1853 William hired ten men to hew stone from the bluffs along the river. He then added stonemasons and carpenters, and a new fort rose in the trading empire that ran from mid-Texas to Wyoming, from the mountains to mid-Kansas. A little smaller than the adobe fort, it had twelve rooms around an interior plaza.

But tension rose between Indians and whites as the numbers of immigrants grew. The Colorado gold discovery heated up the question of who the southern plains belonged to. By 1864 the flame was white hot. Outrages by Indians terrified whites in Colorado and Kansas. In one, a band of Cheyennes wiped out a three-wagon train and its soldier escort. The whites included a husband, wife, and their two children. The Indians emasculated the man before his wife's and children's eyes, brained the children, and gang-raped the woman. She survived long enough to hang herself the next morning. The story may not have been completely true in all details, but all Colorado and western Kansas thought it was.

On November 29, 1864, Civil War hero John Chivington led a regiment of Colorado volunteers to a village of Cheyennes on Sand Creek, about fifty miles northeast of William's fort. William's son Robert had been forced to guide the soldiers. Chivington told Robert as they sneaked forward in the dawn: "I haven't had an Indian to eat for a long time. If you try to fool me, I'll have you for breakfast."

Three more of William's children, George, Charles, and Julia, were in the camp. The Cheyennes had been told by the army to camp there as they would be safe. In the massacre that followed, George was seriously wounded, Charles was captured, and Julia apparently escaped.

Charles, embittered namesake of William's beloved brother, became a brutal, treacherous killer, the worst desperado on the plains. He even tried to kill his father who had disowned him. Fortunately for the whites and for himself, Charles died of malaria in 1868.

William died in 1869, rich and heartbroken.

Suggested reading: David Lavender, *Bent's Fort* (Garden City: Doubleday & Co., 1954).

NAMES ON THE LAND

Bob Dempsey was a controversial man. Some respected him; some called him a horse thief. Some said he was openhearted and generous; others a reckless drunk. All agreed that he championed the Indians and was the best trader on the Emigrant Road that connected the Oregon Trail in Idaho with the goldfields of Montana.

Born in Ireland, Bob came to Canada in 1846 when he was nineteen. He worked his way down the Mississippi River to New Orleans, where he enlisted in the army for the War against Mexico. In spring 1849, he hired on with the Mounted Rifles as a teamster to go to Fort Hall on the Snake River. Discharged a year later when the Dragoons went on to Oregon, Bob used the money he had saved to buy horses and outfit a hunting and trading expedition.

Bob and his partner, Jim Simonds, hunted and traded up the Snake and over the mountains to the Madison, Gallatin, and Jefferson Rivers in present Montana. They were successful, and when they reached Fort Owen in the Bitterroot Valley that fall, they traded their loads of furs to Major Owen.

Bob returned to Fort Hall, outfitted again, and traded the 1850-51 winter on the East Fork of the Snake. Then he set up a trading post at Soda Springs, Idaho, to trade horses with emigrants for their worn out and lame oxen and cattle. These he drove to the Big Hole and Beaverhead Rivers in Montana where they recovered their strength to be returned and traded for what seemed an endless supply of worn out animals from the Oregon trail.

Bob became a close friend of Chief Tendoy of the Lemhi branch of the Shoshones. He married (Indian style) Margaret, a member of the tribe. Bob continued trapping and trading in competition with the Hudson's Bay Company. He became well acquainted with James and Granville Stuart, pioneers of early Montana, and with Johnny Grant, the half-blood foreman for Hudson's Bay. Johnny and Bob's wife were cousins.

The Hudson's Bay Company withdrew from the country in 1861. Johnny Grant stayed to become Montana's leading rancher. By this time Bob was freighting in flour and other goods from Salt Lake City, five hundred miles south. He also farmed and sold farm products to prospectors in Montana. His name still is used for two creeks in his trading area. Dempsey Creek in Montana is near Deer Lodge. Dempsey Creek in Idaho is near Lava Hot Springs, which was, itself, originally called Dempsey.

Suggested reading: Ruth A. Olson and Rebecca Frandsen, "Best Trader on the Emigrant Road," in *True West, v. 27, no. 6* (August, 1980).

BEEF KING OF MONTANA

Conrad Kohrs, six feet, three inches tall, had long arms, and strong muscles rippled down his wide-shouldered back. He moved easily among the group of Montana Territory prospectors that September day in 1862, as they traveled south from Gold Creek. They had heard of the big strike on Grasshopper Creek, a hundred twenty miles away, and once again Con was going over the hill to what might be greener pastures.

It all started in 1850 when fifteen-year-old Con ran away from his Denmark home to sail as a cabin boy on a schooner to South America and then to the United States. He had been a butcher boy in New York City, a grocery clerk in Iowa, a lumberman in Wisconsin, a sausage salesman in New Orleans, and a disappointed prospector in western North America. He had become a United States citizen in 1857. Now he was in Montana, poorly clothed, with little food and completely broke again. He wondered if this was the best he could do.

About half way between Gold Creek and Deer Lodge Valley the prospectors met Henry Crawford who traveled north with fresh news of the Grasshopper diggings.

"Would there be a butcher among ye, lads?" Crawford asked. "Too many are coming to Grasshopper. Faith, I'd rather feed them than scramble against them for a place to seek my treasure."

Con remembered his days in New York City. He remembered the icy mountain streams he'd forded and the cold winds of winter and the hot winds of summer as he sought the elusive color in California and British Columbia. He also remembered chopping away at harsh, rocky soil with blistered hands in the midst of mountain grandeur that he could enjoy only when he looked up to rest his aching back.

"I'm a butcher," he said.

"I'll pay twenty-five a month, and you furnish your own tools."

All Con had was a skinning knife and a sharpening steel. He traded for a scale, a carpenter's saw that would do to cut meat, and a ground-down Bowie knife. Crawford bought three fat heifers and told Con to herd them back to Bannack, the gold camp at the grasshopper diggings.

Con succeeded, even though the heifers tried valiantly and repeatedly to return to their home. Once they got mixed in with a rancher's herd, but with help from a passing horseman Con reached Bannack ahead of Crawford. They rigged up a meat block and a tripod and built a shanty with a brush roof. The first heifer they shot dressed out at seven hundred pounds.

"Can you keep books?" Crawford asked.

"I guess."

So Con became bookkeeper, salesman, and manager, and Crawford rode off to buy more cattle.

Crawford was fond of the bottle and cards, and Con was soon out of inventory. When Crawford returned, he learned that Con had bought a few work oxen, just in from the plains, and even some moose, killed in the mountains. A delighted Crawford quadrupled his employee's pay to a hundred dollars a month.

Beef brought fifteen cents a pound for boiling cuts, twenty for roasts, and twenty-five for steaks. Miners had little time for boiling or roasting, so most of the meat was cut into steaks. Most miners said, "Charge it," and Con's journal soon contained twenty to thirty entries for each day. Crawford hired an assistant, and Con began going out to buy cattle. His first purchase was seventy-five dollars each for ten cows with large calves at their sides.

Henry Plummer's gang of road agents and killers were active that winter. Plummer suspected that Crawford knew about their activities, and their quarrels led to Crawford shooting Plummer in the arm. When Plummer recovered, Crawford fear retribution. He took the company money, leaving everything else to Con, and disappeared. Con was now in business for himself.

Con had many satisfied customers, a shop, and tools, but neither money nor inventory. He borrowed enough to buy sixteen worn-out work oxen, and skillfully traded them for sixteen fat steers. A few days later, he borrowed enough from friends to buy twenty more fat steers. Then Indians stole the entire herd.

Con convinced his creditor friends that their only hope of payment was to loan more money so Con could buy more inventory and stay in business. They came through, and Con began buying from Johnny Grant in Cottonwood, the territory's leading rancher.

Then gold discovery on Alder Creek emptied the Bannack camp. Con, with hundreds of dollars in accounts receivable, looked like he was through. But he formed a partnership with Ben Peel, and Kohrs and Peel set up a meat market in Alder Gulch with five hundred dollars of borrowed money. They soon moved to Summit, where they erected a log building, divided evenly between living quarters and meat market.

Cattle began coming from Utah and Oregon, and Con even bought hogs in 1863 that were driven in from Salt Lake City. By then the partners were butchering and delivering meat during the day and working late every night rendering tallow and making candles which sold for $1.50 a pound. They worked all their meat scraps into sausage. Hides had no value, so they donated them to miners as carpets for their sod-floored shanties.

As the business prospered, Con began buying meat for other butchers.

CONRAD KOHRS

Montana Historical Society

AUGUSTA KRUSE KOHRS

Montana Historical Society

He was on the road much of the time. He usually made the circuit from Virginia City to Bannack to Cottonwood and back — a distance of several hundred miles — in a week's riding. Road agents had become more numerous and bolder, and Con often had to hide from them like a hunted fox. Con became a marked man, not only for the large amounts of gold dust he carried, but also because of his former association with Crawford whom the robbers distrusted.

George Ives and Dutch John Wagoner once followed Con as he left Virginia City with five thousand dollars in his saddle bags. Con was riding Grey Billie, the best horse in his string and one of the fastest in the country. After a scary, fifty-mile ride, Con reached Johnny Grant's house just ahead of the robbers. But he turned his horse in with Grant's horses, and Grant's herder mistakenly drove them to water too soon. Grey Billie foundered and was crippled for the rest of his life. Soon after, Ives tried to outrun a posse but lost that race, too. He was hung on December 21, 1863.

Two road agents were hung on New Year's Day, 1864. Henry Plummer and two more were hung on January 10, and five at one time were strung up on January 14. Although we have no evidence that Con Kohrs was a member of the vigilance committee, and he denied it, his life was certainly much safer by the middle of January. He always referred to January 14 as a "day of few regrets." The vigilance committee hung eight more in the next few days. Some claim that the Plummer gang had killed over a hundred people.

In spring 1864, Con rode to Fort Benton to buy a herd of cattle from the American Fur Company. It had been sold by the time he got there, and he made the round trip of four hundred eighty miles in six days. He kept relay horses stationed where he most often rode, but eighty miles a day even on fast horses is a lot of saddle pounding for six days.

Business continued to increase until Con was buying most of the butcher cattle coming into Montana Territory. Once, he bought four hundred sheep, the first band to arrive from Utah. But miners had little taste for mutton. With no market for the fleeces, Con gave them away for mattresses.

Heavy snows in the fall of 1864 kept most of the wagon trains from entering the territory, and speculators drove up the price of most food and supplies. Con and Peel, with a corner on the meat market, held their prices. Grateful miners called the season a "beef straight winter."

In summer 1865, Con probably rode more miles than any other man in the territory. He owned twelve of the territory's best saddle horses. He particularly enjoyed racing the stage from Virginia City to Helena.

The partnership broke up in summer, 1865, when Ben Peel fell in love. He followed the girl down the Missouri River until he caught up with her in Missouri, where they married and settled down.

Con bought Peel out of the partnership with a solid gold bar, worth seventeen thousand, five hundred dollars. Con wasn't grandstanding with the gold bar. It would be hard for a robber to carry away, and, if the steamer carrying it down the Missouri River sunk, it would be easier to retrieve than sacks of gold dust or coins.

Later that summer, Con bought out Johnny Grant. He paid nineteen thousand dollars for the land, horses, equipment, and cattle. Now a pillar in the community with a thriving meat business, the largest ranch in the territory, and many mining properties, Com began building ditches and storage facilities to sell water to miners and farmers. Dozens of men and several whole families now worked for him on wages.

In 1867, Con decided he needed a wife. His mother and stepfather and a brother had followed him to America, settling in Iowa. Con remembered a lovely girl he had known in the old country, and he learned from his brother that she was also in Iowa. He set out in early December, riding a series of stages and trains to Davenport, Iowa, where he spent the holidays. He learned that the girl, tall, beautiful Augusta Kruse, had moved to Cincinnati. He followed, introduced himself, and on February 23, 1868, they were married at his parents' home in Davenport. They boarded a Missouri River steamer at Omaha on April 16, and reached Fort Benton on June 8.

In years to come Con Kohrs would become close friends with Theodore Roosevelt, Dakota rancher, both before, during, and after his term as president. Marcus Daly, the copper king, was also a close friend.

In the disastrous winter of 1886-87, Con Kohrs lost a half million dollars worth of cattle in one storm. An even greater tragedy was the loss of his son.

Con Kohrs was elected to the Territorial Legislature in 1885, and the state senate in 1902. He died in 1920, aged 84.

This tall, strong, generous, fair-minded man of action, unafraid to borrow money to get ahead, and with friends always ready to loan it, became a commercial giant in Old West history.

Suggested reading: Larry Gill, "From Butcher Boy to Beef King," in *Montana, the Magazine of Western History, v. 8, no. 2* (April, 1958).

LONELY FERRYWOMAN

Emma Batchelor, 21-year-old English woman and a new Mormon convert, was traveling west with a handcart company in 1857 when she midwifed Sister Gourley at the birth of her child. Afterward she helped pull the mother's cart and carried the family's young son across the icy mountain streams. When the company, after losing almost a third of its people, reached Salt Lake, Emma became a servant for one year to Brother Kippen's wife to pay the church for her cost of transportation.

The Kippen family expected that Emma would join it as a plural wife when the year was up. Emma thought differently. She did not like Sister Kippen, and she repulsed every advance Brother Kippen made.

The next December, John D. Lee, a delegate to the legislature from southern Utah, visited the church Emma attended, and she was impressed with the good looking, well-spoken man. Here was a man a girl could look up to! In less than a month Brigham Young pronounced them man and wife.

When Emma and Lee reached his home in Harmony in early February, she met the rest of his family. Earlier wives included Aggatha and Rachel Woolsey, sisters, Lavina and Polly Young, also sisters, and fifth wife, Sarah Williams. Two other earlier wives had already left Lee. After his marriage to Emma, he wrote in his diary: "I believe her intentions real and her integrity true."

Lee's oldest daughter, Sarah Jane Dalton, was about Emma's age. Another wife, Mary Ann Williams, had been sealed to Lee as his legal wife when she was fourteen with the understanding that she did not have to become a wife in fact until she was eighteen and then only if she wanted to. Emma soon learned that Mary Ann and Lee's oldest son, Alma, were in love.

Alma and Mary Ann were married in January, 1859. Earlier, Lee had tried to make love to Mary Ann. When she rebuffed him, he learned that she loved his son, and he agreed to the marriage. Emma rejoiced in the wedding.

She did not rejoice two months later when her husband married Terressa Morse. She shared living quarters with Terressa, who had a bad disposition. The next month their husband went into hiding to avoid arrest for his role in the Mountain Meadows Massacre, which happened on September 11, 1857, before Emma had met him. From then on he divided his time between hiding in the mountains and visiting Harmony and Washington to see his wives and look after business interests.

Lee's role in the massacre is still unclear. But it was clear by October, 1870, that he was to be sacrificed by the Mormon Church to stop any further investigation of its role in the killing. In that month he was excommunicated, and shortly after that Brigham Young advised him to take one or two wives and move out of Utah. Taking Emma and her five children, wife Rachel Woolsey, and two of wife Ann Gordge's children with him, he established a ferry on the Colorado River just south of the Utah boundary. Ann Gordge was one of the wives that Emma particularly liked.

Emma and Rachel had never been close. The bleak countryside and the lack of adult female company led Emma to name it Lonely Dell. The name was later changed to Lee's Ferry.

Emma had another daughter in January, 1872. They named her Dellie after Emma's name for their home. Three months later, Lee took Rachel and Ann's children with him and left Emma and her children alone to operate the ferry and the farm which supported it.

Lee or one of his other wives would return occasionally, but Emma and her children had to operate the ferry by themselves. Almost a hundred wagons were crossed in the month of May, 1873. Emma, pregnant again, had to rely on her thirteen-year-old son, Bill, to help in the October delivery.

This time Emma had another girl, and Bill helped his mother tie the umbilical cord, cut it, rub the little baby with olive oil, sprinkle flour over the navel, and pin on the belly band. Emma warned her son to not let the other children know the details of childbirth. When he carried the placenta out for burial, he was careful that they didn't see. An exhausted Emma asked Bill to not tell the other children about the baby until she had an hour to rest. Emma had been thinking a lot of her old home in England with its damp fog, green grass, and its wonderful queen. She named the baby Victoria in honor of that queen.

Three days after the birth, Jacob Hamblin stopped in. He was a famous Mormon missionary who sometimes quarreled with John Lee. Hamblin admired Emma's courage in running the ferry alone, but he reminded her that church policy required a woman to either leave her husband who had been excommunicated or, at least, quit having his babies. Emma told him plainly that her life was none of his business, and she wouldn't trade the little finger of her beloved husband for a whole regiment like Hamblin!

Lee arrived two weeks later, and a delighted Emma showed him his new daughter. But Lee spent Christmas with Rachel at her home. By this time the church considered Emma the owner of the ferry, since she ran it after her husband had been excommunicated. Once, when Brigham Young's wagon passed a house where Emma was visiting, he had the team slow down while he doffed his hat to Emma to show his respect.

Lee was finally arrested in November, 1874. When Emma heard the news, she explained to the older boys that everything would be different now. The ferry was in her own name, and she expected increasing business as the church sent hundreds of families south to colonize Arizona Territory.

Almost a year passed before Emma could get away to visit Lee in jail. As she rode up, a guard asked, "Who is that good looking woman?"

"Just one of John D. Lee's whores," replied the other guard.

Emma lashed the guard twice across the face with her buggy whip before he could escape her onslaught. Emma couldn't stay for Lee's trial as a date had not been set, and she needed to return to the ferry.

Lee was tried in July, 1875. The jury of eight Mormons and four non-Mormons could not agree. All the Mormons voted to acquit; the others voted for the death penalty. Lee was transported to the penitentiary in Salt Lake City to wait for another trial.

Rachel, in Salt Lake City, got the warden to let her husband work outside on the prison grounds and spend the nights with her. In return, Rachel served the prison as cook and washer woman.

Back at the ferry, Billy was now breaking oxen and had just hauled in two and a quarter tons of supplies without a break down. Emma sent Lee three dollars and asked him to tell his lawyers to hold on, that they would certainly be paid. The boys were fencing the farm, and Emma made seventy-two gallons of molasses from their cane crop.   She planned a visit to St. George to buy more seeds and fruit trees to plant.

Emma had also furnished horses and supplies to a gentile prospector—Wells Spicer, one of Lee's lawyers, who would later become a famous Arizona judge—in return for one-fourth of anything he discovered. Lee did not approve of that transaction.

Lee was released on bail in May, 1876. He visited several of his wives, including Emma. At his second trial on September 11, exactly nine years after the massacre, a new jury found him guilty and sentenced him to death. He was shot by a firing squad at the site of the massacre.

Emma continued to operate the ferry for three more years. In 1879 she agreed to sell it to the Mormon Church for a hundred head of cattle. She only got sixteen, and they were delivered grudgingly. Three months later she married Frank French, a prospector who had often bought supplies from her and had eaten an occasional meal with her family.

Emma, a faithful wife to a strange, controversial man, had operated a ferry for seven years at one of the West's most historical river crossings. The place is still called Lee's Ferry, Arizona.

Suggested reading: Juanita Brooks, *Emma Lee* (Logan: Utah State University Press, 1975).

MERCHANT OF AMPLE MEANS

Ledyard Frink was a merchant of "ample means" in Martinsville, Indiana, when he and his wife, Margaret, decided to follow the gold rush to California. The couple, in their thirties, had been married eleven years. They had no children of their own, but were raising an eleven-year-old foster child.

Their wagon, "suitably built" for the 1850 journey, had storage bins below the floor for their provisions and baggage. Containing an India-rubber mattress for air or water (they used air and they inflated it every night), plus a feather bed and pillows, the wagon served well as a bedroom when closed up at night. They lined the interior with green cloth, pleasant on the eyes, and added side pockets for small conveniences such as mirrors and combs. A cast-iron cooking stove, lashed on behind, and two India-rubber, five-gallon water bottles completed the outfit.

Margaret wrote, "We knew nothing of frontier life, nor how to prepare for it. But, nothing daunted, we prepared to go alone, as no one else was going from our part of the country."

At first they planned to take only their foster child. But then Ledyard agreed to take Aaron Rose, a young clerk in his store, who wanted to go west. While they waited for Rose to get ready, Ledyard and Margaret practiced driving their four-horse team.

When Ledyard learned that lumber cost well over a hundred times as much in California as in Indiana, he bought enough for a modest home and hired carpenters to cut the pieces and mark them for assembly. Then he sent the lumber down the White, Wabash, Ohio, and Mississippi Rivers to New Orleans and around Cape Horn to Sacramento.

The Ledyards were sure of two things: they would need a supply of acid to fight scurvy, and they would need flour scoops to pick up their gold. The decided to buy the scoops after their arrival, but they laid in a big supply of vinegar and pickles.

They started on March 27 and would stay in inns and farmhouses until they reached the Missouri River. At their first night's stop, the landlady of the farm they chose stuck her head out of the barn and shouted, "We're having trouble with a cow, and I've got no time for strangers." Ledyard went to the barn showed the "milkman" how to handle the cow, and the highly pleased landlady let them stay in the house that night.

When they reached Springfield, Illinois, they heard that a California emigrant had been murdered that day about ten miles ahead. That night they got out their Colt's revolver to make sure it was in working order.

They reached St. Joseph on April 23, where they waited fifteen days for the grass to grow. Not sure they had enough people to cross dangerous

Indian country, they took on a Mister Avery, who was looking for a ride. This required buying another wagon, a light one pulled by two horses.

They drove north to cross the Missouri at Bullard's Ferry, ten miles south of the Platte. The stories they heard about deeds of violence and bloodshed weighed heavily on Margaret as they waited to cross. The first night after crossing, they camped on a knoll. Margaret got out her spyglass and saw mounted Indians in the distance. (Probably Pottawamies whose only offense against whites was begging.) They checked their armament (one rifle and one revolver) and worked quickly to prepare their camp for defense.

Just then five Michigan men drove up and asked if they could join their camp. Margaret felt greatly relieved as the men corralled the wagons, staked the horses safely inside, checked their firearms, and organized watches for the night. Apparently Ledyard was the only one who got any sleep. Margaret wrote, "For my part, I did not change my clothing during the entire night, neither shoes nor bonnet."

Five days later the Frinks joined in with other wagons for traveling and security. Ledyard was elected captain. The next day, they met the trail angling up from the St. Joseph crossing of the Missouri. Long trains of white-topped wagons were visible for miles ahead and behind.

"It seemed to me," Margaret wrote, "that I had never seen so many human beings before." She saw a cart drawn by two cows, a man on horseback with an ox to carry his provisions and blankets, and another man pushing a wheelbarrow loaded with his supplies.

After they passed Ash Hollow and moved up the North Platte, the axle broke on their light wagon. Ledyard remembered seeing an abandoned wagon back down the trail. He rode back alone, removed the axle, and used it to replace the broken one.

On June 17, near present Casper, Wyoming, they ran into a heavy snowstorm. The next day they snowballed each other until ten o'clock, when the snow started melting.

Even though they were two weeks ahead of the average Oregon or California Trail emigrant, Mr. Avery left them on the Sweetwater River, saying he could beat them to California on foot. They gave him everything he could carry on his back, and he set out for the last fifteen hundred miles. (He did beat them to Sacramento by two weeks. After staying a month, he was so homesick he took a steamer home.)

They made good use of their water bottles crossing the desert at night from South Pass to Green River. Ledyard took sick with mountain fever during this passage. The next few days were the darkest part of their journey.

The Frinks had no trouble with Indians or cholera. Margaret described the Humboldt as the most miserable river on earth. Yet they had no trouble following it, finding feed for their horses, and reaching the Carson River. They enjoyed the clear, cool water as they climbed into the Sierras, which they crossed on August 30 through snow fifteen feet deep.

They reached Sacramento on September 7, an early end for a journey of 2418 miles. Margaret called on a Methodist minister to learn the prospects for starting a Baptist Church. She became a founding member.

They rented a house in Sacramento. Ledyard built a dining table and benches, set up a kitchen, and they hung up a sign, "Frink's Hotel." Margaret did the cooking, while Ledyard sold their horses, harnesses, and equipment, using the money for tableware and furniture. By the end of their first month, they had cleared two hundred dollars.

Then cholera broke out, and both Frinks and their foster son fell ill. But Margaret hired a boy and directed him in keeping the business open. When they recovered, the Frinks leased a larger house and continued their business.

Ledyard bought three cows. Milk was worth two dollars a gallon, but they put it on the table, free to their customers. Ledyard had to buy ten more cows to keep up with the growing business. The next spring, they bought an established dairy with all its equipment. After supplying the hotel, they sold forty dollars worth of milk each day.

They sold the hotel and bought another dairy. They paid their milkers eighty dollars a month and hired Aaron Rose, their former clerk who had not found any gold, at a monthly salary of one hundred fifty dollars just to collect their money from customers.

The Frinks bought two lots at the corner of M and Eighth Streets. It took just a week to set up the pre-cut home they had shipped around Cape Horn. A larger home soon replaced the modest cottage.

Their foster son eventually settled down in business in Sacramento. Their former clerk, Aaron Rose, returned to Martinsville with three thousand dollars in gold dust.

The Frinks never regretted what Margaret called "the prolonged hardships of their toilsome journey with its happy ending in the fair land of California."

This remarkable couple, naive but indomitable, left their mark on California. They found gold without digging it out of the ground.

Margaret died in 1892, aged seventy-four. Ledyard lived eight more years.

Suggested reading: Margaret A. Frink, "Adventures of a Party of Goldseekers" in Kenneth L. Holmes, (ed.) *Covered Wagon Women, v. 2,* (Glendale: Arthur H. Clark Co., 1983).

THE GREAT CONDENSER

Carnation milk, the best in the land,
Comes to the table in a little red can.
No tits to pull, no hay to pitch,
Just punch a hole in the sonofabitch!

Grateful cowboys sang that verse in bunkhouses from Texas to Montana, from the Dakotas to Nevada. No longer did they have to milk cows so the rancher's wife would have butter for their bread and milk for their coffee. You can't milk on horseback, and it's a nuisance job anyway. A man should throw a rope over a cow brute's head; not pull on her private parts.

As happy as they were with condensed milk, probably few cowboys knew that the inventor was a religious teetotaler, a schoolteacher and surveyor with just one year of schooling, and one of the most important builders of early Texas, although usually hidden in the background.

More importantly, Gail Borden was a tinker, a workbench mechanic like the bicycle men who made the world's first airplane. When his fertile brain seized on an idea about doing something, he kept trying until he got it done, unless—as sometimes happened—a better idea came along to capture his attention.

Twenty-six-year-old Borden was a county surveyor in southwestern Mississippi when he married sixteen-year-old Penelope Mercer in 1828. Much later, when he was married to his third wife, Borden said that Penelope was the only woman he ever loved. 1828 was the year his father moved from Indiana to Texas. Gail's brother, Tom, was already there, a member of Stephen F. Austin's colony. Gail had been in Mississippi six years, and Texas looked a lot more inviting. He followed his father and brother in 1829.

Gail and Penelope reached Galveston Island, once the lair of pirate Jean Lafitte, on December 23. Daughter Mary was born the next day on Christmas Eve.

Texas, the size of France, had two thousand Anglo Americans. Mexico granted Gail a league of land, 4428 acres on the Colorado River. Surely this was a land of opportunity! He began farming and stock raising, and practiced surveying on the side.

Mexico granted land only to Roman Catholics, but didn't have enough priests available to enforce the requirement. Like many of the colonists, the Bordens were outside the pale of any organized religion. But the Mercers were a family of Baptist preachers, and on February 4, 1840, almost four

GAIL BORDEN

Courtesy, The Borden Company

years after Texas had won its independence, Gail and Penelope were baptized in Galveston Bay. It was the first baptismal service in the Gulf of Mexico west of the Mississippi River. The memory of that day would sustain Gail through difficult days to come.

Borden became an important leader in early Texas, serving as collector of customs in Galveston. A leading newspaper publisher, he printed leaflets opposing the Mexicans and cheering the colonists who escaped from Santa Anna's soldiers. He created the phrase, REMEMBER THE ALAMO. He had been the surveyor of the Stephen F. Austin Colony and later laid out the City of Houston. He was trustee of the Texas Baptist Education Society which, among other things, founded Baylor University.

Gail's and Penelope's first child died shortly before its fourth birthday. By 1844 they had another daughter and four sons. In March of that year, their third son, Stephen F. Austin Borden, not quite five, died of yellow fever. Six months later, Penelope died of the same disease. Gail's new religious faith saw him through the grief.

By the 1840s Borden had become fascinated with the idea of condensing. While walking through his cluttered Galveston yard in 1844 with the new assistant pastor of the Presbyterian Church, he gave examples of his new interest:

"If I were advising an absent son how to live, I'd forget long lectures and refer him to a New Testament chapter for the theory and to Proverbs for the practice."

"Lovers no longer write poetry; they condense what they have to say into a kiss."

"Condensation has even spread to eating. People used to spend hours at a meal. Napoleon took twenty minutes; I can do it in fifteen."

"I've even learned to condense my sleep into six hours in which I get more rest than most people do in ten."

Later Borden would say that he wanted to condense anything that people ate: "I mean to put a potato into a pill-box, a pumpkin into a tablespoon, the biggest watermelon into a saucer."

Penelope's death left Borden lonely and confused. He had five children, the oldest thirteen. Five months later he married a Mrs. Stearns, about whom we know little except that she derided her husband's habits and tinkering and probably died about 1856.

When Borden saw Penelope die of yellow fever, he resolved to search for a cure, even though medical men had failed. The disease always left after the first frost of autumn. "Why not refrigerate it out of existence?" he thought. He calculated that a dozen ounces of ether would chill an average-sized person as though exposed to thirty or forty degree weather and would keep the person there for a week. But by the time he had built his first refrigerator he was off on a new idea, a meat biscuit.

He also invented the terraqueous machine, a wind-powered vehicle that traveled on land and water. It crashed on a demonstration trip, and he turned his full attention to the meat biscuit.

By 1849 the war with Mexico had ended, and a large area in the west with names like New Mexico, Utah, and California belonged to the United States. Gold had been discovered, and people by the tens of thousands would be moving west. The recent Donner-Reed tragedy had highlighted the danger of running out of food. Could food be condensed to reduce the problems of long supply lines and slow mules? Gail Borden was determined to try.

He remembered that the Comanche Indians of Texas had mixed pulverized, dried buffalo meat with crushed hominy and mesquite beans into a product that could be eaten dry or moisturized into a cake. For traveling, they pressed it into a buffalo intestine, which they wore as a belt. Borden chewed some of the compound and started thinking.

By 1850, Borden had a patent on his meat biscuit, the United States Army was interested, and Borden had a crew of six Germans—an engineer and five laborers—working for him. Eleven pounds of meat was condensed into one pound of extract, which was then mixed with flour and baked, or made into a syrup, pudding, or pie.

At first the Army loved it, and officers wrote glowing reports. They said soldiers didn't crave more solid food and even dispensed with coffee. With financial help from Dr. Ashbel Smith, formerly surgeon-general of the Texas Army, Secretary of State of the Republic, and now one of the state's principal leaders, Borden built a factory on Galveston Island. He appointed agents from coast to coast, and his meat biscuit won a gold medal at a world's fair in London. The *Scientific American* called the biscuit "one of the most valuable inventions that has ever been brought forward."

But a later report by the army was less than enthusiastic, and the biscuit's initial popularity dimmed. Borden refused to give up. He wrote: "If God gives me two more years, Texas, if not the world, will see that I have not lived in vain."

God gave him twenty more years, and he fulfilled his prediction with milk, not the meat biscuit. The kindly Galveston Sunday School teacher had often given children milk as they traveled west with their parents. He scalded it to make it keep longer, but he was still not satisfied. He noticed that Texas women cooked their fruit in sugar syrup to keep it from spoiling. "Why can't I do that with milk?" he asked himself.

Another story tells that Borden put a pan of milk on the stove one evening for a warm milk toddy. Then he went off, following another of his brainstorms, and he returned hours later to find a sticky white paste — his first condensed milk. Borden knew it would be difficult to retain the purity and freshness of the most delicate of foods for weeks or longer without losing its life-sustaining properties. It became a challenge suited for the determined dreamer, often seen pacing the streets of Galveston, his head down, his eyes on the ground, his mind absorbed in his latest idea.

Borden had learned with the meat biscuit that he needed eastern capital. He also needed access to laboratories and scientists. Until then his laboratory had been his cellar, his instruments the process of trial and error. He returned to New York, his birthplace, and settled in Brooklyn in 1852. In 1856 he opened a factory in Connecticut. It failed. He tried again the next year and failed again. In 1858 he tried the third time. Then the Civil War produced a demand for condensed milk, and Borden soon had two factories in Connecticut, two in New York, and one in Illinois. He licensed other companies to use his discoveries.

Borden returned to Texas in 1871. He built a school for freed black people and another for white children. He organized a day school and a Sunday school for black children. He helped build five churches, maintain two missionaries, and support teachers, ministers, and students.

Borden also invented the lazy susan, which still is an important part of many kitchens.

The Borden company became the world's largest dairy business. From there it grew through PVC (Polyvinyl chloride), adhesives for both the lumber industry (plywood glue) and consumers (Elmer's Glue), instant coffee and snack foods, and hundreds of other products to became a world giant with thirty thousand employees. Its Elsie the Cow is one of the world's most recognized trademarks. The company is a monument to a man of little education but great determination.

Gail Borden died in January, 1874. He was buried in White Plains, New York. He wrote his own epitaph:

> I tried and failed,
> I tried again and again, and I succeeded.

Borden County in west Texas, and Gail, its county seat, are named after the man who refused to give up. Most of the residents are ranchers and cowboys. Some may be old enough to remember the ditty about the little red can.

Suggested reading: Joe B. Frantz, *Gail Borden, Dairyman to a Nation* (Norman: University of Oklahoma Press, 1951).

DOAN'S CROSSING

In spring 1872, brothers Jonathan and Calvin Doan left Wilmington, Ohio, looking for a fresh start in life. Their two young nephews, cousins Robert Doan and Corwin Doan, rode with them to Fort Sill, Indian Territory. The five-year-old fort sat in the midst of the Kiowa-Comanche Reservation. The Indian Agency was two miles south, and varying numbers of hostile Indians inhabited semi-permanent villages near the agency. The four Doans worked at odd jobs and then got permission from the Indian agent to open a small hide and fur trading post.

The Indians began bringing in buffalo hides and smaller pelts to trade. Jonathan contracted to buy the hides of the seventy to eighty cows that the agency gave to the Indians each year. Corwin helped butcher, to make sure the Indians didn't steal the hides. Since the hides came on the cows, Indians may have thought they already belonged to them.

Trading was brisk, but with little profit. The Doans hired teamsters to freight the hides to St. Louis. The teamsters took advantage of their position, and charged prices the Doans thought exorbitant.

However, the brothers made many friends among the Indians. On busy days rows of babies on cradle boards lined the store walls, and happy puppies scuffled as giggling women traded and warriors smoked and talked. The traders kept the coffee hot, with brown sugar and molasses to mix with it. Candy bits, broken crackers, and sugar lumps were given away generously. No one left without clutching a "sweet" in the hand.

The Doans presented the chiefs with tobacco, beads, and shiny metal for making arrowheads. Big Bow, a Kiowa chief, had been in the habit of leading his warriors up to the agency and arrogantly asking if their "presents" would be handed over of if they would be forced to take them. When he tried that with the Doans, the brothers said they would hand the goods over if the Indians would point out what they wanted.

Later, after Big Bow and Corwin had become friends, the chief said, "Indians are fools, not smart like white man You handed the goods over that day, but Washington took it out of our pay."

Big Bow missed the irony that the Doans submitted the bills for the "free" goods to the government.

Business increased, but so did trouble with the Indians. Angered at the lack of annuities at the agency, they began raiding into Texas, killing and plundering along the Red River. When no troops chased them, they rode arrogantly into Fort Sill, challenging the small command. Some Indians suggested that the Doans move their post south to the Red River.

Corwin was ill, Robert was homesick, and the Indians were in disarray, spending too much time raiding and too little hunting and collecting pelts. The brothers decided to move. They put their nephews on an eastbound stage and set out for the crossing the Indians had suggested.

They looked the crossing over, but the buffalo hunters they depended on were deeper in Texas, so they went northwest into the Texas Panhandle and set up a post near present Memphis. Business was disappointing, and they moved again. Still they did not prosper, and Jonathan reconsidered the crossing of the Red River that the Indians had first recommended.

By then the Doans knew that large trail herds of cattle were moving north on the Chisholm Trail, crossing the Red River at the Red River Station, about a hundred twenty miles (measured in a straight line) downstream. But that crossing was deep and dangerous, with quicksand. The bottlenecks sometimes held up crossings for weeks, and in late summer, 1874, some trail herds left the Chisholm Trail and cut northwest for an alternate crossing. They pushed eleven thousand cattle across at the very place the Indians had recommended. The water was shallower, the current slower, and the bottom free of sand.

The next spring, Jonathan and Calvin picked a spot a mile and a half south of that crossing. With two hired hands, they cut down hackberry and Chinaberry trees, trimmed the limbs away, and cut the trunks into equal-length pickets. They set the pickets vertically in the ground, chinked between them with sod, and covered the building with a sod roof. The twenty-four by thirty-foot building had a dirt floor and a buffalo-hide door. One half was filled with groceries, ammunition, and whiskey. The other side, with a fireplace, was where they would live.

That winter they started trading with stragglers from the cattle herds, buffalo hunters, and Indians. By spring 1876, the brothers had to ship in supplies from Denison, Sherman, and Gainesville. Nearly sixty thousand cattle passed the Doan store that year. It was the best crossing for a hundred miles in either direction. Without quicksand, the bottom hardened as cattle passed over, and the crossing got even better.

In normal weather the river was three feet deep and a hundred feet wide. But rains could swell it to a treacherous depth of fifteen feet, and herds would still have to wait.

Business prospered, and in 1878 Jonathan sent for his two daughters, still in Ohio. By then Corwin had married, and he was ready to come west again. He brought his wife and baby along with Jonathan's daughters.

The trail at the crossing came to have many names. In Texas, it was usually called the Great Western Trail, but sometimes the Texas Cattle Trail, the Lone Star Trail, and the Dodge City Trail. In Indian Territory it was the Trail from Texas. As it neared Kansas, it was the Dodge City Trail.

Indian Territory contained many gun runners, whiskey peddlers, and hostile Indians. The only places with lawful authority were Forts Sill and Supply. Beyond them, the cowboys were on their own. Herds were often held up at the crossing to rest the cattle, apply road brands, and prepare for the worst. Such waits increased the business coming to the Doans.

A post office opened in 1879 with Corwin Doan as postmaster. He had asked for the name Baldwin Springs, but the Post Office Department said too many towns were named for springs. They named it Doan.

In 1880 the Doans replaced the picket house with an adobe building. Later that year, Jonathan and Calvin sold out to Corwin, and they built a new store several miles south at Eagle Flats. Corwin immediately put up a sign: C. F. Doan's and Company — Good Cigars and Bad Whiskey. That year, two hundred thousand head of Texas cattle crossed at Doan's Crossing. Corwin's family grew and he hired more employees. He also built a large storehouse for supplies.

One of Texas' worst drouths came in 1882, and even more cattle were trailed through Doan's Crossing for the railroad at Dodge City. That was the summer of the Dry Thunder, when lightning flashed and thunder roared out of clear skies. Lightning struck Doan's store as eleven trail herds waited to cross. One of the largest stampedes in Texas history followed. One hundred twenty cowboys took ten days to collect the cattle and sort them out.

A town began growing around the store. By 1885 it had three hundred people. It became home to many teamsters who freighted between Doan's store and Wichita Falls. The town had a blacksmith and wagon repair shop, a hostelry, several eating places, and a hotel of sorts where lonely cowboys could buy female company. The Cowboy Station, with drinking and dancing, did a big business. But the heart of the town was the trading post, built by the Doan Brothers and sold to their nephew.

In 1888 more cattle left Texas by Doan's Crossing than on the Chisholm Trail. The future of Doan's store looked bright, but the end was already beginning. Trail herds had started to dwindle. The Fort Worth and Denver Railroad built through Eagle Flats (present Vernon), bypassing Doan's Store. Residents began moving away until only Corwin Doan's family remained. He no longer sold groceries by the wagon load, and had to depend on his farming for a living. Then the Cherokee Strip was opened to settlement in 1893, and the homesteaders with their fences brought an end to the Great Western Cattle Trail. The last herd went through in 1895. All that is left now, besides written memories, are two granite monuments, one on each side of the Red River.

Suggested reading: Angie Irons, "Doan's Crossing," in *True West, v. 36, no. 11* (November, 1989).

JACKASS MAIL PIONEERS

George Chorpenning started east from Sacramento on May 1, 1851, with pack mules carrying two hundred pounds of mail for Salt Lake City. He and his partner, Absalom Woodward, had a contract with the government to provide monthly mail service between the two cities for $14,000 a year.

In crossing the Sierras, Chorpenning and his men had to pound the late winter snow down with wooden mauls so their mules could travel. After sixteen days of struggle they crossed Carson Pass and reached Carson Valley in present Nevada. There they arranged to establish a mail station at Mormon Station, later called Genoa.

They followed up the Humboldt River, and struggled through more deep snow at Granite Pass in the Goose Creek Mountains of northwestern Utah. They traveled north of the Great Salt Lake and reached Salt Lake City on June 5, just five days late. The return trip with westbound mail was easy.

"Looks like we made a good deal," Chorpenning told Woodward when he returned to Sacramento. "That fourteen thousand a year is as good as in the bank."

A few threats and rifle shots from hidden Shoshones were just minor nuisances for the next two passages. Woodward took the August train out. Ambushed by mounted Shoshones near present Carlin, Nevada, he fought his way over Emigrant Pass to escape.

Back in Sacramento by fall, Woodward also led the November train east. He left on the first of the month with four men and $5000 in gold coin plus the mail. They were across the Sierras in a week, but then had to rest their animals in the Carson Valley for another week. They met the westbound train two weeks later near Emigrant Pass. Both trains were, of course, two weeks behind schedule. Woodward's party said goodbye, and rode into the Great Basin winter, never to be seen alive again.

The remainder of the 1851-52 winter was a disaster. Chorpenning's men could not cross the Sierras in December or January. He re-routed them south to San Bernardino and up the Mormon Trail to Salt Lake City. The February mail crossed the Sierras at the Feather River Pass and reached Salt Lake City in sixty days. The men suffered terribly when their horses were frozen to death in the Goose Creek Mountains, and they had to travel the last two hundred miles on foot. The March mail was also re-routed down the coast to San Pedro and then followed the Mormon Trail.

That spring Shoshones were exchanging twenty dollar gold pieces at Utah trading posts, and the story began to be pieced together. Woodward had escaped when the Shoshones attacked along the upper Humboldt, but he died of wounds and exposure at the Malad River, almost three hundred miles east of where he had been wounded. His men had been killed outright or run down by the warriors.

As the 1852-53 winter approached, the government raised Chorpenning's compensation to $50,000 a year, and gave permission to carry the winter mail through Los Angeles. Then the eastbound mail to Carson Valley was carried from Placerville by men on skis, the most famous of whom was Snowshoe Thompson. Chorpenning had taken the May 1, 1852, mail himself, learning his partner's fate upon his arrival in Salt Lake City.

In 1854 the Utah-California mail route was changed to run down the Mormon trail the year round from Salt Lake City to San Diego. Again, Chorpenning was the successful bidder for $12,500 a year. Unexpected Indian resistance led to pay increases until Chorpenning received $30,000 a year.

By 1858 California wanted daily mail service from the midwest, with as little elapsed time as possible. John Butterfield got a $600,000 annual contract for twice-weekly service along the long southern route that connected St. Louis to San Francisco through El Paso and Yuma. Then Chorpenning got a $130,000 annual contract for weekly deliveries along the Utah-California road through Carson Valley. He changed from pack mules to coaches, and the east and westbound coaches were expected to meet at Gravelly Ford, near present Winnemucca.

The first trip went well, but Indian raids and the icy slopes of Granite Pass led Chorpenning to seek a more southern route. He started southwest from Salt Lake City and passed south of the Great Salt Lake to the Ruby Valley of Nevada. The next year he followed an even more direct route from the Ruby Valley to Carson Valley. Later the Pony Express would follow Chorpenning's route all the way from Salt Lake City to Placerville.

Although Chorpenning had pioneered the routes eventually followed by the Pony Express and by the first railroad to cross America, he fell on hard times. Congress reduced his contract, and then refused to appropriate funds for it. In 1860, the government nullified Chorpenning's contract and awarded it to the Pony Express. All of his stations and stock were taken over by the Pony Express without compensation.

George Chorpenning died on April 3, 1894. Not a single western newspaper favored him with an obituary. The Jackass Mail pioneer had been forgotten by the people who had benefitted from his courage and fortitude.

Suggested reading: LeRoy Hafen, *The Overland Mail* (Cleveland: Arthur H. Clark Co., 1926).

BETTER THAN SHOVELS AND WHEELBARROWS

David Staples started his journal on April 16, 1849: "Left the city of Boston, a member of the Boston and Newton Joint Stock Association, bound for Cala-fornia for the purpose of bettering our conditions on money matters and seeing the country."

The 25-member group had planned well. They bought a bark, the *Helen Augusta,* loaded it with tools and provisions, and sent it ahead around Cape Horn. Leaving their families behind, they traveled by train, lake steamer, and river boats to Independence, where they bought riding mules and started across the plains. They drew lots for their mounts. Staples, one of the tallest at 6 feet, got the shortest mule. His feet barely cleared the ground as the little Spanish mule tried in vain to buck him off.

Death came quickly. The brother of Staples' young bride died of cholera in Kansas. But there was no more trouble. When they reached San Francisco in early October, they learned that their bark's cargo was worth a small fortune. After selling the ship and cargo, each man had a generous and unexpected stake.

Staples tried prospecting on the Mokelumne River. Within a few days he knew that shoveling sand and pushing a wheelbarrow were not how he wanted to better his condition on money matters. He bought a string of pack mules and started freighting from Stockton to the mines. By February, 1850, he had enough money to buy 17,000 acres of rich land along the lower Mokelumne. By August he had a 3800-square foot house, barns, corrals and outbuildings, roads and levees, and a profitable ferry. Then he returned to Massachusetts for his wife and baby daughter.

Staples had learned to work when young. Orphaned at eleven, he worked in a cotton mill to help support four younger brothers and sisters. At thirteen he agreed to work three years for a farmer for board and room, three months of school in the winter, and a new suit of clothes at the end of his term. The three years produced disappointment. Farm work left no time for school. The suit of clothes was a shabby thing, outgrown by an older boy in the family.

A kindly shoemaker took Staples in as an apprentice at sixteen and encouraged the young man to learn to read and write in night school. Two years later he took up the mechanic's trade, which he followed until leaving for California at twenty-four.

After Staples got his family to California in January, 1851, he continued to prosper and his ranch made money. He even trapped bears, which he sold to promoters of bull and bear fights.

In 1852, Staples and two other men convened the first Republican convention in San Joaquin County. Eight years later Staples was a delegate to the national convention where John C. Fremont, the previous candidate who lost to James Buchanan, asked him to present Fremont's nomination again. But Staples helped turn the tide for a tall, plain-looking young man from Illinois.

Staples went back east for Lincoln's inauguration. Apaches in New Mexico and hooligan Texans, looking for Yankee Republicans, delayed his stage. By the time Staples reached Washington, Lincoln was in office and seven states had seceded.

Later that year, Staples sought his party's nomination for California governor. He lost to Leland Stanford, who went on to win the election. Stanford appointed him to the Board of Port Wardens in San Francisco, one of the leading appointed positions in the state.

Four years later, Staples' term ended. At forty-one he was out of a job for the first time in thirty years. But not for long.

A group of San Francisco businessmen had formed a new insurance company. Ten percent of the profit was designated for the volunteer firemen in the city. The company was called the Firemans' Fund Insurance Company. Each policy holder got a plaque to put on his building. It didn't take the fireman long to figure out where to concentrate their efforts in the large fires that swept the city from time to time. The company prospered, but its president died.

The directors asked Staples to take over the company. He ran it for thirty-four years, and he ran it well. Under his leadership, the company was one of the few that paid claims in full after the Chicago fire in 1871. The Boston fire the next year almost broke the company. But by the Virginia City fire in 1875, Staples had made Firemans' Fund one of the leading insurance companies in the world.

It still is.

Suggested reading: William Bronson, *Still Flying and Nailed to the Mast* (Garden City: Doubleday & Co., 1963).

WHEELBARROW JOHNNY

Nineteen-year-old John Studebaker said, "We need capital. Two wagons in one year won't get it."

"With you joining us," older brother Henry said, "we'll be able to build more."

"Yes," said middle brother Clem. "You're a good man with the tools, Johnny. The three of us could soon have a nice little wagon company. Maybe even bring Pa in. Give him some lighter work than the hard blacksmithing he's done so long."

The boys father, a German blacksmith and wagon builder, had been unhappy with prospects in Pennsylvania. He moved to Ashland, Ohio, in 1835 when John was two. His family had increased by three in 1848 when he moved again, still looking for a place where his sons would have a better chance in life. They settled near South Bend, Indiana.

Four years later, Henry and Clem had started on their own, calling their company H & C Studebaker, wagon builders. But they only sold two wagons their first year.

"They're paying two dollars a cord for firewood in town," John said, responding to his brothers. "I'll stick to cutting wood."

Now, in 1853, Henry and Clem tried again to bring their younger brother into the company. But a wagon train was being formed to follow the California gold rush. "They say they pick it up right off the ground," John told his brothers. "When I've got enough for the capital we need, I'll come home."

John agreed to build a wagon, give it to the train, and drive it to California in return for his transportation and his food. The boys' parents had raised them in a strong religious faith (now Church of the Brethren, closely related to the Mennonites) and his mother told John to "be a good boy and don't gamble."

"I won't, mother," he assured her.

John's mother sewed sixty-five dollars of his savings into a hidden money belt to help him get started in California. The sixteen South Bend wagons joined with twenty-two Chicago wagons. When they reached the Missouri River at Council Bluffs, John learned about three card monte.

It didn't look like gambling. Certainly he could pick out a correct card among three which had been shuffled before his eyes and dealt face down. But unless John could see better than the dealer could shuffle, he had to lose with an even payoff on a bet that he had one chance in three of winning. His sixty-five dollars soon disappeared. He resolved to never gamble again. He still had fifty cents, which lasted until he reached

California.

After five months they reached Old Dry Diggings, just beginning to be called Hangtown (now Placerville). One of the welcoming crowd offered a job to any wheelwright or man who could build wagons.

At first John refused the offer, saying he had come to California to dig gold. But a man in the crowd told him that not everyone found gold, and many were hungry. Remembering Council Bluffs, John reconsidered and took the job.

"What we need is wheelbarrows," John's new boss, H. L. Hinds, said. "Besides regular smithy work, I'll pay ten dollars for every wheelbarrow you build. I've already got twenty-five orders."

John took two days to build his first wheelbarrow. The green wood made it crooked, and some miners laughed. But John built tools that he needed, and the next wheelbarrow was much better. Within two years he had saved three thousand dollars, and gold country prospectors called him Wheelbarrow Johnny.

John figured the wagon company back in South Bend would need eight thousand dollars in capital. He had become acquainted with Mark Hopkins, determined to start a store when he had enough gold, and Phillip Armour, who sold fresh meat from a wagon until he could open his first butcher shop. The three shared similar dreams about business in America.

In fall 1857 John's savings had reached seven thousand dollars. His brothers were then producing a dozen wagons a year, and they agreed that eight thousand dollars would be enough additional capital. The next spring, John returned to South Bend with the money. He bought out Henry, who only wanted to be a farmer and did not share his brothers' views about the manufacturing business. John and Clem continued building wagons.

John's next visit to Placerville came in 1912. Government contracts in the Civil War had helped the company become the leading manufacturer of farm wagons. It also made buggies, freight wagons, fire engines, hearses, and ambulances. Shortly after John became president, the company began building gasoline automobiles. At the time of his visit to Placerville, the value of John's share in the company was estimated at eight million dollars.

Wheelbarrow Johnny had been right from the beginning about the need for capital. He knew where to get it, but he didn't find it exactly as he expected.

Suggested reading: Edwin Corle, *John Studebaker, an American Dream* (New York: E. P. Dutton & Co., 1948).

GOLD RUSH TRADER

John Sloane Collins was twenty-seven in 1864 when he left Council Bluffs with six wagons loaded with merchandise for the Montana Gold Rush. He took a ferry across the Missouri River to Omaha and met his brother, Gilbert, who had recently come from Illinois. The brothers formed a partnership to deal in leather and saddlery goods.

Gilbert returned to Illinois to buy more merchandise, and John headed on west with six wagons, one pulled with four horses, the others with two-horse teams. He traveled with a larger train of about two hundred wagons, led by Captain Thomas Prowse. Near Fort Kearney and approaching the area where hostile Indians might attack, they picked up another wagon. It was driven by a two-hundred pound Irish girl who only gave her name as Jane.

"I've me own team and kin take keer of meself," Jane said. "I'd like to go wid ye."

"All right," Prowse said. "We got a hundred and fifty men. I reckon you can bake our bread, mend our trousers, and sew buttons on."

Jane smiled as though to say, "not likely."

They told Jane to stay near the middle of the train. They had no trouble with Indians, but they had to camp once between a marsh and a small lake and use backfires to avoid a prairie fire. Jane did her part by carrying water to the men as they built and extinguished the backfires.

As they drove on through ashes falling from the sky, they did see a scalped man with an arrow through his body. They met a friendly Indian who told them a Sioux war party had attacked some Pawnees, and advised them to watch their livestock carefully. They visited Fort Laramie a few days and were impressed with the well-dressed Indian women.

They left the Oregon Trail at the Snake River, turning north near Fort Hall. They had to dig through eight feet of snow in late May, but had no more trouble, reaching Virginia City on June 12.

Laborers made five to eight dollars a day, and hired miners made ten. Gold at eighteen dollars an ounce was the currency, although greenbacks at fifty percent discount were accepted.

Collins saw Jane a few days after they reached Virginia City.

"Have you found your gold mine yet?" Collins asked.

"Lord bless you, darlin'. I worked in a hotel for thirty-five a week and then went to washing clothes. I already got seventy-five in dust in me buckskin bag. I'm going to invest in a washboard and tub and get rich."

Most of the mining was at Virginia City, but nearby Alder Gulch would produce the richest placer mines in the world. Within a year it had a population of six thousand. Collins found a cabin halfway between Virginia City and Alder Gulch.

He witnessed the longest prize fight in the West, the 185-round contest between Con Orem and Hugh O'Neil. Fought in January, 1865, in twenty-five below zero weather, the fight ended in a draw.

Flour was normally thirty-five dollars a 96-pound bag. When merchants withheld it from the market to drive the price up, the bread and flour riots of Virginia City followed. A mob led by Paddy Ryan searched houses, basements, and hiding places of all kinds, confiscating exactly half of what they found. The price of a bag of flour dropped from $130 to $45 in twenty-four hours.

Collins was an avid hunter. Later, from 1872 to 1881, he would be post trader at Fort Laramie where his closest hunting companions were General George Crook and Webb C. Hayes, son of the president. He described the display in a Virginia City meat market at Christmas, 1864. They had a half dozen buffalo, a dozen mountain sheep, a dozen each of elk, deer, and antelope, a half dozen each of mountain lions and grizzly bears, plus many small black bears and innumerable grouse.

Besides selling the supplies he had hauled in, Collins began buying gold dust for a banking firm, Nowlan and Weary. He also served as agent for a stage line. When gold was discovered at present Helena in summer, 1864, Collins moved there to open a branch for his bank. Soon he was making a salary of $1250 per month.

In February, 1866, Collins moved to Silver Bow and opened a store with his last wagon load of goods. He still had twenty bags of flour, plus canned goods, bacon, sugar, coffee, and gold pans, picks, and shovels. Shovels sold for an ounce of dust ($18).

There were only two buildings in town, one of them a store. That storekeeper tried to get Collins to charge seventy five dollars for a bag of flour. Collins refused, setting the price at fifty. When the miners learned of Collins' prices, they took two wagons to the competitor's store, loaded up all the goods they could carry and paid one-fourth the asking price. The competitor left, and Collins had the market to himself.

In July Collins sold the rest of his stock and returned to Omaha, a two thousand mile ride in an open boat down the Missouri River. He and his brother eventually had branch stores in Cheyenne, Wyoming, and in Miles City, Billings, and Great Falls, Montana. They made the Collins saddle into the most popular cowboy saddle in the world.

Suggested reading: John S. Collins, *My Experiences in the West* (Chicago: R. R. Donnelley & Sons, 1970).

RED, WHITE, AND BROTHERHOOD

The West's most famous cattle trail was named after a merchant who never raised a cow. Jesse Chisholm's cattle were the steers he yoked to pull trade wagons.

Chisholm was born in Tennessee in 1805. He grew up with his mother's people, the Cherokees. An aunt married Sam Houston, who had been governor of Tennessee. Houston persuaded Chisholm's people to move west to Indian Territory before the army forced them out of Tennessee.

By 1830 Chisholm was trading in partnership with James Edwards at Fort Gibson, near present Muskogee, Oklahoma. Their trading post was the last supply stop for travelers bound from Fort Smith to Santa Fe, and the business prospered. Wild Indians on the plains further west hated to come into the timbered country to trade. So Chisholm loaded his pack train with beads, paints, and brightly-colored cloth, and he took his mule-back department store out to his customers. He traded with Comanches, Kiowas, Caddoes, and Wichitas for furs, buffalo hides, and wolf skins. He never dealt in liquor.

In 1836 Chisholm married his partner's half-Creek daughter, Eliza. To be nearer the Indians, Chisholm and Edwards then moved their trading post to Little River, about five miles from present Holdenville, Oklahoma.

Chisholm earned a reputation among both Indians and whites as an honest, industrious trader, respected by all. The Indians called him the man with the straight tongue. He became their friend and counselor. He hoped that Indians and whites could learn to live together in brotherhood and peace.

Eliza died in 1846, leaving her husband with two young sons. The next year, Chisholm married again. He and his second wife had four more children.

Chisholm learned to speak fourteen Indian languages and dialects. He interpreted for the army, and he provided help at major peace conferences.

He sometimes bought Texas and Mexican children, who had been captured by Comanches and turned into slaves. He returned the children to their families when he could. When he could not, he raised the children as his own.

In 1861 pressure from Southern sympathizers forced the civilized Indians out of Indian Territory. By then Chisholm had moved his trading post to Council Grove, on the North Canadian River, a few miles west of present Oklahoma City. From there he led Shawnees, Cherokees, and Creeks north over two hundred miles to settle on the Neosho River in Woodson County, Kansas. But even there they found no peace, as guerrillas raided reds and whites alike. So Jesse Chisholm led the Indians on west, where they settled at a Wichita camp on the Little Arkansas River, near present Wichita, Kansas.

The southern Indians built cabins and corrals, and lived with the Wichitas for the rest of the Civil War. Chisholm, who had been adopted into the Wichita Tribe, became recognized as the leader of the settlement. A creek near the large encampment is still called Chisholm Creek.

When the war ended in 1865, Chisholm led his people back to Indian Territory. The 220-mile journey ended at the Wichita Agency, near present Chickasha.

Two years later, when Texas cattlemen trailed the first herds north to railroads, they followed the wagon ruts left by Chisholm and the Indians. The trail became popular with the cattlemen because it had less timber, better grass, fewer large streams to cross and more small streams for water. Also the cattlemen were taxed less by civilized Indians, and raided less by wild ones. The cowboys began calling their route the Chisholm Trail.

Chisholm's name was eventually given to the extension of the trail as it continued into South Texas. By then a cowboy could ride the Chisholm Trail for eight hundred miles. The trail from Wichita to Fort Worth was later followed by the Chicago, Rock Island, and Pacific Railroad, and, after that, by United States Highway 81.

It is doubtful that Jesse Chisholm ever knew that his name had been given to the most famous of the cattle trails. He died in 1868, the year after the cattle began moving north.   He got food poisoning from bear grease, melted in a brass kettle.

Jesse Chisholm never carried a gun and was never wounded, either by bullets or arrows. All people considered him a good samaritan. Respected and loved by both races, his tombstone says, "No one ever left his home cold or hungry." He could ride all over Indian Territory with no fear of any man, red or white.

T.U. Taylor, *Jesse Chisolm* (Bandera, Texas, Frontier Times, 1939).

THE HERCULES OF EXPRESSMEN

Dave Butterfield, no relation to his namesake John of Butterfield Overland Mail fame, was also in the transportation business. Dave had prospered as a Denver grocer during the Colorado gold rush. In early 1864 he moved to Atchison, Kansas, built a large home, and set up a commission merchant business. He became the agent for Missouri River packet boats, which hauled freight from St. Louis to Atchison.

The established trade route followed a circuitous path from Atchison to Denver. Freight wagons and stages traveled northwest to the Little Blue River, followed it to its headwaters, and crossed over to the Platte. Then they followed the military road along the Platte and the South Platte, leaving the latter stream to head southwest to Denver.

New York millionaire Ben Holladay had taken over the old Butterfield Overland Mail and moved it north to the Platte River route. Then he added the Leavenworth and Pike's Peak Express, and he owned the largest one-man business in the world.

Dave Butterfield listened to the complaints of freighters and stage passengers about the roundabout travel to Denver, and he decided to open up a direct route in competition with Holladay. He created the Butterfield Overland Dispatch to follow up the Kansas and Smoky Hill Rivers directly from Atchison to Denver. His route would cut almost a hundred miles off the longer one to the north.

Butterfield advertised his new venture throughout the East. The shorter route was discussed over lunches from Washington to Boston. The nation's three largest express companies invested in the enterprise. New York banker Edward Bray was named president, and Butterfield became the superintendent. By June, 1865, three million dollars had been subscribed, half of it already paid in.

Butterfield convinced his backers that their wagons could haul freight west at half the prices charged by Holladay and haul passengers east at one-third those prices. He built stations, and bought twelve hundred mules and hundreds of work oxen. The first wagon train left on June 24 with seventy-five tons of freight and a military escort of two hundred fifty soldiers. Several engineers went along to remove obstructions and select sites for future trail stations.

Butterfield also bought twenty new coaches and set up a twice-weekly stage schedule to Denver. The first stage pulled in to Denver on September 23, with Butterfield aboard.

Denver residents greeted the stage and their former merchant with an enthusiastic celebration. They displayed a banner saying:

"Westward the Course of Empire Takes its Way. The energy of our old townsman, Col. D. A. Butterfield, proves him the Hercules of the Expressmen. Welcome, Dave and your express."

The crowd cheered when Butterfield announced plans to open daily service to Santa Fe and tri-weekly service to Salt Lake.

But Butterfield worried about Indian attacks as the troops which had been called east to fight the Civil War were slow in returning. Indian attacks in central Kansas forced Holladay's Leavenworth and Pike's Peak Express north. Fort Kearny, Fort Sedgwick, and smaller camps and outposts provided protection in the north that was absent further south. In early October, 1865, Indians attacked and burned one of Butterfield's stages. The next month the station at Bluffton was burned to the ground, and two stock tenders killed.

Attacking Indians were not Butterfield's only problem. Holladay cut his stage fares to meet the new competition. The only profitable run for Butterfield was the short one from Denver to the gold camps at Central City. Holladay had been charging ten dollars for that run. Butterfield charged six. Then Holladay reduced his fare to one dollar, which Butterfield could not match.

Dave Butterfield never got a mail contract, and he never got adequate military protection for his stages. He did make one run to Denver in less than four days. Holladay's line required six. For a short time the newspapers praised Butterfield's fast stages. He had encouragement from Eastern express companies who wanted a western competitor to Holladay, but they fell through when Butterfield needed their business most.

By March, 1866, the Butterfield Overland Dispatch was broke. At a secluded table in Delmonico's restaurant in New York, Holladay sat down with the president and main investor in Butterfield's line. When the lunch ended, Holladay, the King of the Plains, owned still a bigger stage and freighting business, and Dave Butterfield was out of a job.

But the transportation bug had bitten Butterfield. He moved to Mississippi and organized a railroad. Later he moved to Hot Springs, Arkansas, where he built and operated a horse-car line. The Hot Springs venture seemed to prosper, but Butterfield got in a quarrel one day with an employee. He cursed the employee, and the man picked up a neck-yoke and beat his boss to death.

Dave Butterfield's star shone brightly in western transportation, but not for long.

Suggested reading: Frank Root & William Connelley, *The Overland Stage to California* (Columbus: College Book, 1950).

CHATTEL MORTGAGE

In spring 1873 the 7th Cavalry moved from its duty stations in Kentucky and the mid-south to three forts in Dakota Territory. Six years of campaigning in the southern plains had made the regiment and its glory-seeking field commander, George Armstrong Custer, famous. When the regiment moved out of Fort Lincoln for a summer scout on the Yellowstone River, people wondered what exciting news would follow.

A young man in Beulah, a small hamlet in eastern Iowa, wanted to be part of the regiment's history. He got an army contract to provide hay to the cavalry horses at Fort Lincoln the following winter.

The young man had nerve and ambition, but no money. But he had the next best thing — a banker willing to back him. The Beulah banker—we don't know his name, either—explained the need for the security of a mortgage to protect the bank's investment. So the young man got the money he needed to buy mules and hay making equipment, and the bank got its chattel mortgage.

As soon as the young contractor had his mules and machinery together at Fort Lincoln, he started cutting prairie grass hay in the meadows west of the fort. The cavalry was still out on its scout, but the young Iowan thought Indians would never bother anyone so close to a fort, even an unguarded one. He was wrong. The temptation was too much for a marauding band of Sioux, when they saw the mules grazing at night, unrestrained. They stole the entire herd.

The young man had no money of his own. He wrote the banker that he was sorry and told him where the bank could repossess the mower, hay rake, and wagons. Then he disappeared from history.

The next spring the Beulah banker traveled over to Yankton and bought passage up the Missouri River to Fort Lincoln on the *Josephine.* On the trip up he discussed his mission with the skipper, Captain Grant Marsh. He explained the bank's loss and his intention to see what he could salvage from the unfortunate venture. When he finished the sad story, Captain Marsh asked him if he had taken the matter up with the military authorities with whom his customer had contracted.

"Oh yes," the worried banker answered, the pain evident in his voice. "I have written to general Custer, asking him if he did not think that the Indians would give those mules up to me if they knew I held a chattel mortgage on them. I am not connected with the army, and I have never caused the Indians any harm."

He shook his head and looked at Marsh, his eyes filled with sadness. "But the general has never replied to my letter."

The story about the Iowa banker's loss and his views about the influence of a chattel mortgage on hostile Indians made the rounds at frontier army posts and campfires. A few years later it surfaced again with Captain Marsh. This time he was operating the *Yellowstone* on the Missouri with General Nelson Miles as one of his passengers. Miles, one of the most experienced army officers on the frontier, had played the leading role in fighting Indians after the Custer disaster.

As Marsh and Miles enjoyed themselves in conversation, the *Yellowstone* came around a bend and they saw a beautiful horse grazing quietly a short distance from the river. The day was clear and warm, the prairie grass was green, and the sunlight glistened on the horse's sleek legs and well-muscled rump and shoulders. A heavy strip of timber behind the horse provided the background for a perfect picture of the West.

"Should I pull to the bank and stop?" Marsh asked Miles. He grinned but his voice sounded serious. "Looks like we could capture a fine looking horse. We have room on the boat to take him along. He'd make you or one of your officers a fine mount."

Marsh had not skippered boats through hostile Indian country for nothing. He knew full well that the horse was a decoy, put out by Indians hiding in the timber. They hoped to stop the boat so they could raid it.

Miles, also, had a wealth of experience in fighting Indians. He had not acquired his skill by reading anthropology books. He solemnly studied the horse and the strip of timber for a moment and then turned to Marsh with a smile.

"Yes, Grant," he said, "that sure is a fine animal. One of the best I've seen. You're right. He'd make me or one of my men a superb mount. I can just see myself riding off on the next campaign on his back." He looked again at the timber and shook his head ruefully. "But I'm afraid there may be some Indians around who hold a chattel mortgage on him. They probably wouldn't want to give him up."

The two experienced westerners laughed together as the vessel, out in the middle of the river, kept chugging forward.

Suggested reading: Joseph Mills Hanson, *The Conquest of the Missouri* (New York: Murray Hill Books, Inc., 1946).

TEN YEARS IN NEVADA

Most women who went west in the frontier days were wives, teachers, or prostitutes. The few who were different included Mary McNair Mathews.

In 1869 Mary, a 35-year-old Civil War widow, took her nine-year-old son and left their New York home for Virginia City, Nevada. Mary's younger brother had been killed, and she wanted to determine the value of the mining properties in his estate. She sold her hoop-skirt factory to raise travel funds and journeyed west on the train.

She stopped in Buffalo to consult with ex-President Millard Fillmore about legal matters. Fillmore refused to charge a fee; in fact, he gave Mary ten dollars to help with her expenses. For the next seven or eight years, Mary would struggle with lawyers in her attempts to realize something from her brother's estate. Anything she recovered must have been miniscule compared to the results of her own efforts in getting ahead.

Mary and her son left the train at Reno. They reached Virginia City by stage on August 30 with just twenty-five cents left in their pockets. Before the day ended, Mary found work as a seamstress for a dollar a day, plus board and room.

She increased her income by nursing sick children and taking in laundry. She also started a private school. Mary, who had studied at Oberlin College for three years, had twenty students, each paying fifty cents a week. In addition she tutored a group of adults in reading and writing.

Mary increased her production when she bought a sewing machine. She also rented a four-room house for twelve dollars a month. She and her son Charles used two rooms. She fixed up the other two to rent out at twelve dollars a month each.

After a careful study of her accounts, Mary realized that the boarding house and the sewing produced the most income for the time spent. She discontinued the laundry and the school. She also developed a profitable child care business. Customers booked her several weeks in advance. About this time she began trading profitably in mining stocks. Many of her tips came in dreams.

Mary bought a house for five hundred dollars to stop paying rent. She had the house moved to the back of a lot in Virginia City and contracted for the construction of a store building in the front with a boarding house above. Impatient with the builder's performance on the fifteen hundred dollar contract, Mary paid him off and finished the construction herself.

She rented out her old house for twenty-five dollars a month and moved into the boarding house. She began making twenty-six beds a day and doing the washing and ironing for her roomers.

The disastrous fire of October, 1875, missed her property. She made sixteen extra straw ticks, spread them on the floor, and opened her doors to the homeless.

Mary's apparently fruitless attempt to recover anything from her brother's estate had included a five week trip to California shortly after she moved to Nevada. She visited Dutch Flat, Gold Run, San Francisco, Stockton, and Sacramento. In later years she kept trying to find lawyers to sue mining magnates on a contingent-fee basis. Her failure to find one produced frustration that ended when she met a lawyer referred by a friend.

Mary had been sick for several days. She was barely able to sit up when her friend brought the lawyer in. She got the papers she had collected, gave them to the lawyer, and sat back down.

"I don't know," the lawyer said after examining the papers. "I don't see much of a case at present, but I'll come back when I have more time and look at them some more."

"Very well," Mary said.

"You look pale. What's the matter?"

"I'm sick from a poisoned finger."

The lawyer did not take the hint to leave. Mary got to her feet and began re-arranging some books on a table. The lawyer followed her, and tried to kiss her.

Mary sprang back from his would-be embrace before, as she said, "his poisonous lips had polluted her face by their touch." She grabbed a clothes brush and flung it at his head.

"Go," Mary shouted, "you contemptible villain. Never dare enter my presence again! I can get decent lawyers to transact my business."

"What a fury! A moment ago you looked as if you were going to faint, and now you look as if you could kill half a dozen men."

Mary threw a scissors at him, breaking off one point. When her friends asked her about the scissors later, Mary said grimly, "I bit it off one day in a fit."

Mary and Charles, by then a San Francisco actor, returned to New York in 1878. She left instructions with an agent about handling the dividends from her handsome fortune in stocks. After several months visiting her family, she had to return for a short time to make sure her instructions were being followed. Mary didn't have much patience with fools.

Suggested reading: Mrs. M. M. Mathews, *Ten Years in Nevada* (Lincoln: University of Nebraska Press, 1985).

BUSINESS SECRET AT ADOBE WALLS

The buffalo hide industry started in 1871 when twenty-year-old Wright Mooar, hunting in Kansas, shipped fifty-seven hides to his brother John in New York. John did some advertising with a Broadway parade that caught the eye of a Pennsylvania tanner. The tanner bought the hides and ordered two thousand more. Then John joined his brother in Dodge City.

The brothers were Vermont-born Yankees , experienced at business. John was more interested in the marketing end; Wright would handle the production.

Other buffalo hunters moved to Dodge City, and, in 1873, three-quarters of a million hides were shipped out after hunts to the north. Hunting south of the Arkansas River had been reserved for Indians under the Medicine Lodge Treaty.

By 1874 few buffalo could be found north of the Arkansas, so the hunters started moving south. But now each man carried a cartridge filled with cyanide so he had a quick death alternative to the slow torture he could expect if captured by Indians. The Indians depended on hunting for their food and shelter, and they knew that their rights to hunt south of the Arkansas had been secured.

A colorful group pulled out of Dodge City that spring, moving one hundred fifty miles southwest to the Canadian River in the Texas Panhandle. Charlie Myers moved his entire fifty thousand dollar operation and set up a trading headquarters close to the hunters. Besides the Mooar brothers, there was young Billy Dixon, a West Virginia native, considered one of the best marksman on the southern plains, and Billy's even younger friend, twenty-year-old Canadian Bat Masterson.

Dixon and Masterson kept to themselves, thinking the older hunters were a bunch of misfits and outlaws. Some of them had been loners so long they quit using their real names. So Shoot-'em-Up Mike, Light-Fingered-Jack, Prairie-Dog-Dave, and Dirty-face Jones were among the fifty or so hunters and skinners.

The motley caravan of thirty wagons reached the Canadian River in Hutchinson County, Texas, and set up their post a short distance northeast from the ruins of an ancient Spanish settlement called Adobe Walls.   That settlement had been wiped out by Indians many years earlier. About thirty-five years before the buffalo hunters arrived, William Bent had built a trading post at the place where the hunters stopped. Five-foot-high ruins of walls were all that remained of that post.

Soon after their arrival, the merchants had four buildings up, each made from vertical logs set in trenches with sod chinking and heavy sod roofs. Myers built his store at the northeast corner of a large corral, and Tom O'keefe built his blacksmith shop at the south end. Jim Hanrahan built a saloon next to O'Keefe. Charlie Rath's store, the farthest building south, included a restaurant leased to Bill Olds, whose wife was the only woman in the group. Some of the hunters wanted to bring a few of Dodge City's saloon girls with them, but Myers, with the largest investment in the enterprise, firmly said, "no."

By May 1 the trading post, also named Adobe Walls after its two predecessors, was open for business for the two hundred hunters operating in the area. Before the end of the month, Indians attacked Joe Plummer's hunting camp and killed Dave Dudley and Tommy Wallace. The Indians scalped and horribly mutilated their victims. They propped up Dudley's and Wallace's heads so they could see themselves being castrated and watch their bodies bleed to a slow death. Then two more hunters, Antelope Jack Holmes, an Englishman, and a German, Blue Billy, were killed.

On June 18, Amos Chapman, an army scout based at Camp Supply, arrived with a six-man soldier escort and alarming news. He said the army had information that hostile Kiowas and Comanches were planning an attack on Adobe Walls on June 27, the morning after the next full moon. The four merchants who got the news, Rath, John Mooar, Myers, and Hanrahan, kept it secret, afraid the hunters might pull out, leaving them with no customers and no one to help defend their post. No one knows why they kept the news from blacksmith O'Keefe and restauranteur Olds.

John Mooar left the next day to bring in his brother's hunting camp. They returned in five days, after skirmishing with a large band of Indians. Then the Mooar Brothers, Rath, and Myers all pulled out for Dodge City with a load of hides. Of those left at the post, only Jim Hanrahan had knowledge of the impending attack.

On June 26 the Shadler Brothers, Ira and Shorty, pulled in with a load of goods. They had passed the merchants' wagons on the way in, but weren't told of the expected attack. That night Hanrahan agonized over his options. If he said nothing and no attack came, no harm would be done. But if the attack caught them unprepared, they would certainly all be killed. On the other hand, if he told the others, they might hang him for keeping the secret until it was too late to get away.

Sometime after midnight Jim Hanrahan shot his pistol into the air. Two men sleeping in his saloon jumped awake, and Hanrahan shouted, "Clear out, the ridgepole is breaking."

Believing the noise that awakened them was the ridge pole cracking, the men set to work, not noticing that the pole appeared undamaged or wondering why Hanrahan was awake and fully dressed at two a. m. By the time the pole was replaced, half the men in the post were awake, but Hanrahan saw some returning to their bedrolls.

"Free drinks on the house," Hanrahan announced. Most of the hunters accepted, although Bat Masterson was a little young for rotgut whisky at three in the morning. He settled for coffee.

Billy Dixon was outside straightening up his bedroll with Bat Masterson watching just as dawn broke. They heard a rumble of galloping horses and looked up to see the Indians charge. Bullets kicked up dust around them as they ran back into the saloon. The defenders thought the Indians would just try to run off the horses, so the direct attack on the buildings surprised them.

Indians pounded on windows, and their half-white war leader, Quanah Parker, tried to break down one of the doors by backing his horse into it. But Andy Johnson, a Swedish carpenter, had reinforced all the doors with cross planks, and the door held.

The defenders hurriedly stacked breastworks of barrels, sacks of grain and flour, and other supplies against the walls, and began firing from windows and from holes punched through the sod chinking. The Shadler brothers, who had spent the night in their wagon, were the first killed. This left twenty-seven whites, many of them fighting in the underwear they were wearing as they crawled out of their bedrolls. Six men plus Mrs. Olds fought from the Rath store. Nine fought from the saloon. Eleven fought from the corral and the Myers store.

Their initial effort to storm their way into the buildings having failed, the Indians withdrew and considered their next step. Then the big buffalo guns began finding their marks and emptying saddles. Some Indians dismounted to take up positions behind fences and wagons to pour their bullets into the post.

One hostile kept blowing a bugle. But when he approached the Sadler wagon to ransack it, he was killed. Years later, Quanah Parker said the man was a deserting soldier from a cavalry regiment.

Someone yelled from the Myers store that Billy Tyler, a young freighter who had arrived the night before, had been hit. The boy was a close friend of Bat Masterson, who jumped out a window and dashed to the store. Unfortunately the boy died shortly after.

By late forenoon, the men in the saloon were low on ammunition. Hanrahan and Dixon crawled through a window and ran to the Rath store for a new supply. Hanrahan carried the ammunition back alone, as the people in the store, the smallest group, begged Billy Dixon to stay with them.

By noon, the Indians—estimated at seven hundred—had lost dozens of men, and Quanah Parker had been wounded. Now some expressed doubts about the power of Isa-Tai, their medicine man. They dismounted and held a council out of sight of the buildings. As they talked, Isa-Tai's horse fell to the ground, a bullet in its forehead. It was, of course, a stray bullet, but the thunder-struck Indians believed whites could hit targets they could not even see.

Looking at his dead horse, Isa-Tai said sadly, "Whites have strong medicine. Maybe shoot today and hit brave tomorrow."

After that, the Indians kept up a distant siege and killed the rest of the animals, but by four o'clock the attack was effectively over. Later that evening three men rode into the post and were surprised to learn that a battle had been fought that day. They had seen no Indians. After dark, using one of the recently-arrived horses, Henry Lease, armed to the teeth, rode out for Dodge City.

The next day about twenty warriors appeared on a distant ridge, east of the post. Some of the men persuaded Billy Dixon to demonstrate his fabled marksmanship. He agreed and carefully positioned his heavy rifle on a solid rest. He adjusted for wind and the extreme range and slowly squeezed the trigger. Some of the Indians later reported that as they watched the buildings in the distance, they saw a puff of smoke. Then a warrior named To-hah-kah fell from his horse, and after that they heard the gun fire. The Indians contradicted each other on whether the warrior was killed or merely stunned.   After the Indians left, the hunters measured the distance from Dixon to his target. It was exactly 1,538 yards, almost nine tenths of a mile. The hunters always called it Billy's one-mile shot.

A few days later, William Olds climbed a hastily-built observation tower to watch a distant band of Indians. Climbing down in a hurry, he accidentally shot himself in the head and fell dead at the feet of his horrified wife.

The merchants gave up the post, taking their liquor, blacksmith tools, supplies, and dreams of profits back to Dodge City. Behind them, drying on the corral pickets, they left the heads of twelve Indians whose bodies had not been recovered by their comrades. The best estimate on Indian dead and wounded was seventy.

Then the army allowed the Indians back to collect the bones of their dead. The Indians found the heads of their comrades staring across the plains with ghoulish, lipless grins. They burned the post to the ground.

That was the end of the Adobe Walls buffalo hunting station.

Suggested reading: James L. Haley, *The Buffalo War* (Garden City: Doubleday & Co., 1976).

GREAT MEN THINK ALIKE

Hiram Sibley, a machinist in New York, met Samuel F. B. Morse at President William Henry Harrison's inauguration in 1841. Morse impressed Sibley with his new inventions in telegraphy. Sibley bought some of the earliest patents and organized the New York and Mississippi Valley Printing Telegraph Company. Later, he and his friend, Ezra Cornell, organized the Western Union Telegraph Company.

Cornell had started out as a carpenter in Ithaca, New York. When the panic of 1837 cost him his job, he bought the rights to sell a plow in Maine and Georgia. He walked to Maine, covered the state on foot, walked to Georgia, repeated the performance, and then walked home. He helped design a ditching plow to use in laying underground pipelines, and was then hired to supervise the laying of an underground telegraph line from Washington to Baltimore. From then on his interests turned to the telegraph.

In the meantime, Edward Creighton, thirteen years younger than Sibley, also got interested in telegraphy. Creighton, the son of Irish immigrants, had gone to work as a teamster at fourteen to help support his family. Eventually he became a contractor. After he built a stage highway from Wheeling, West Virginia to Springfield, Ohio, he went west to build telegraph lines. He settled in Omaha with younger brother John. Edward built a telegraph line from St. Joseph to Omaha, and then became general manager of Western Union.

In 1860, with civil war threatening, communication became critical between the nation's governmental and industrial centers in the east and its mining centers in the west. At that time, St. Joseph and Sacramento were linked by the Overland Mail, which carried bulk mail through in three weeks. A few dozen brave boys in the Pony Express could carry small letters from one city to the other in ten days in good weather and fifteen in bad. The nation needed better communication.

That summer Edward Creighton rode a mule from Omaha to Sacramento to examine the proposed route. He returned to tell Sibley, company president, that he could build the line.

Western Union's directors did not have the vision of its president and its general manager. Sibley and Creighton resigned and said they'd build the line alone. They formed the Pacific Telegraph Company and started to work. They agreed with a west coast company, which was already building east from Placerville, that the first one to reach Salt Lake would get the largest part of the government-offered $40,000 bounty.

A line had already been built from Omaha to Fort Kearney, Nebraska. Sibley took charge of construction from there to Julesburg, and

Creighton worked from Julesburg to Salt Lake. One of the worries was the reaction of the Indians. The year before, the builders to Fort Kearney had used electrical shock on chiefs to convince them to leave the wire alone. But as Sibley's crew neared Julesburg, an unnamed warrior who, as he put it, "had been down to the states," convinced his comrades that the wire was not to be feared. Anticipating uses in constructing tipis and tethering horses, they cut down a long section of wire at O'Fallon's Bluffs (near present North Platte) and galloped north toward their village on the Blue Water.

It was a hot day, and an electrical storm overtook them. Their treasured wire suddenly acted like a devil, knocking many of the Indians off their horses. They gave no more trouble, although occasionally part of a pole would be cut down for firewood. But the Indians left the wire alone.

Sibley and Creighton had over twice as many miles to build as the Californians, and they did not start until July 4, almost two months after the Californians began. In a race that would be repeated eight years later in railroad construction, Sibley and Creighton beat the Californians by two days, reaching Salt Lake on October 24, 1861. They had won the major part of the forty thousand dollar bounty.

President Lincoln and the California governor exchanged congratulatory messages, bells rang, and guns sounded in celebration from coast to coast. Not celebrating, of course, were Russell, Majors & Waddell. After its short, courageous chapter in Western History, the Pony Express was now out of business.

Creighton and Sibley got rich. Three years later, they merged their new company with Western Union, and they got even richer. Creighton invested in gold and silver mines and in a Western Nebraska cattle ranch. Soon he was Omaha's wealthiest citizen. He had very little education, and he was a devoted Catholic. He often said he wanted to start a Catholic university in the West. His fortune, augmented by that of his younger brother, created Creighton University in Omaha.

Sibley's main interest was in agriculture. He created experimental farms to improve plants of all kinds. He operated the largest farm in New York. By 1888 he owned more acres of improved property than any other individual in the United States. Sibley was also interested in higher education, as was his lifelong friend, Ezra Cornell. Together, they founded Cornell University in Ithaca. Sibley's fortune was used to create the Sibley College of Engineering there.

Three men — Creighton, Cornell, and Sibley — created two universities, one in the east and one in the west.

Suggested reading: Alvin F. Harlow, *Old Wires and New Waves* (New York: D. Appleton-Century Co, 1936).

NORTHERN EXPANSION

After four attempts in 1857 and 1858, a telegraph cable was finally laid across the Atlantic Ocean from Newfoundland to Ireland. Twenty-seven days of jubilant message transmission ended suddenly when the cable fell silent.

Nothing more had been done by February, 1861, when a meeting of two remarkable men led to an attempted cable crossing of the Pacific. One man was Perry McDonough Collins. Fifteen years before, Collins had left his job in a New York law office to work for a shipping company in New Orleans. There he met William Gwin, who would become one of California's first two senators. Gwin believed it was the manifest destiny of America to dominate the North American continent, and Collins quickly converted to the same belief. Like eighty thousand others, he headed west in the 1849 gold rush.

Collins practiced law for a time in Sonora, California, and also went into several business ventures in Tuolumne County. He and Gwin formed the American Russian Commercial Company with a visionary plan to build farming and sawmill colonies in Russian America—present Alaska—and also to ship ice from there to San Francisco. None of the northern plans worked out, but they showed the way Collins could dream.

The Russians dreamed also. Tsar Nicholas I hoped to cash in on trade with China after that country was forced to open its ports to foreign nations. He wanted to expand trade and Russian influence down the Amur, the river flowing east from central Siberia to the Pacific, often called the "Mississippi of Asia."

Senator Gwin and New York Senator William Seward had watched the Russian expansion, noting that it paralleled America's own expansion to California and Oregon. They got Congress to finance a survey of the northern Pacific Ocean, looking toward commercial expansion to that region. The survey ended in 1855, and Collins read its report carefully. It confirmed his view that the Amur was the route through which American commerce could best penetrate northern Asia.

Collins met with President Pierce, and, in 1856, was appointed American consul for the Amur region. Collins charmed the Russians, and was, in turn, impressed with their country. By 1859 Collins was convinced that a telegraph could be built across British Columbia and Russian America. With two short underwater crossings at Bering Strait and Anadyr Bay, the cable company could connect with a Russian telegraph at the mouth of the Amur. Then three great nations, America, Russia, and China, would be in direct communication with each other.

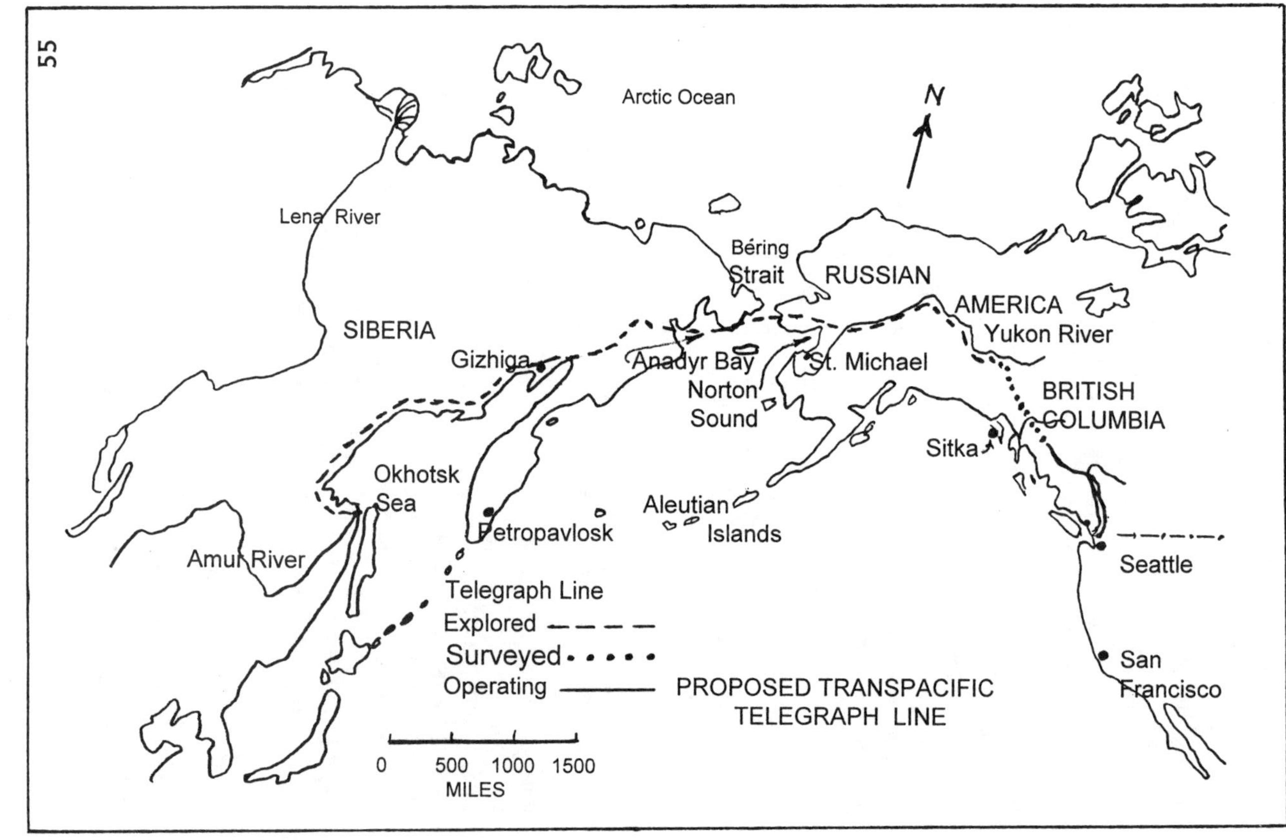
Arctic Ocean
N
Lena River
Béring Strait
RUSSIAN
AMERICA
Yukon River
SIBERIA
Gizhiga
Anadyr Bay
St. Michael
Norton Sound
BRITISH COLUMBIA
Sitka
Okhotsk Sea
Aleutian Islands
Petropavlosk
Amur River
Seattle
Telegraph Line
Explored
Surveyed
Operating
PROPOSED TRANSPACIFIC
TELEGRAPH LINE
San Francisco
0 500 1000 1500
MILES

Then came Collins' meeting in February, 1861, with Hiram Sibley, the other big dreamer. Sibley had used his position as builder of a short telegraph line in the East to assemble a group of companies, then working to span America from east to west. Sibley became president of the combine, the Western Union Telegraph Company. It didn't take Collins long to interest Sibley in an international cable connection across the Pacific, to be built in cooperation with Russia. It could make Western Union a world power. In October that year, just eight days before completion of the coast to coast connection to San Francisco, Sibley wrote Collins that if the Russians gave a right of way across Russian America, he could complete the Pacific crossing in two years. He was probably champing at the bit to get started.

But the Civil War had started, Siberia was a long way away, and Congress had no time or money to spare on building a telegraph line to Asia. Collins, however, would not give up. In 1863 he became vice consul in St. Petersburg, with the primary purpose of getting Russian cooperation for the telegraph line. By January, 1864, he had permission to cross British Columbia and an agreement with Russia that they would extend their lines to the mouth of the Amur. They, of course, gave permission to cross Russian America and that portion of Siberia needed for the line. Now Collins, the government negotiator, moved into the background, and Sibley, the telegraph executive, took over.

Sibley hired Charles Bulkley, former army officer in charge of military telegraphs in the Southwest, as chief engineer. By fall, 1864, most of the workers had been hired. With separate exploring crews working in British Columbia, Russian America, and Siberia, the company had to buy eight river and ocean boats to supply the crews. The Navy furnished an armed vessel for protection.

Western Union had already built a line from San Francisco to Portland with plans to extend it through Seattle to New Westminster, the capital of British Columbia. In April, 1865, the line had crossed the Fraser River, and the first news telegraphed to British Columbia was the assassination or President Lincoln. Construction continued up the Fraser River. Poles were set about 175 feet (thirty to a mile) apart. By early September they had reached Quesnel, 450 miles from New Westminster.

But from Quesnel to the Yukon, the land was known only to Indians and men of the Hudson's Bay Company. The explorers found that their maps were often wrong. Finally they got a Nechako Indian woman, Too-gum-a-hen, to draw a much better map, and they followed it northwest, establishing winter quarters—which they named Bulkley House—at the north end of Takla Lake. The river the line followed before crossing the Skeena River is now called the Bulkley River. Their 1865-66 winter quarters were over four hundred miles from the nearest post office, with only two houses

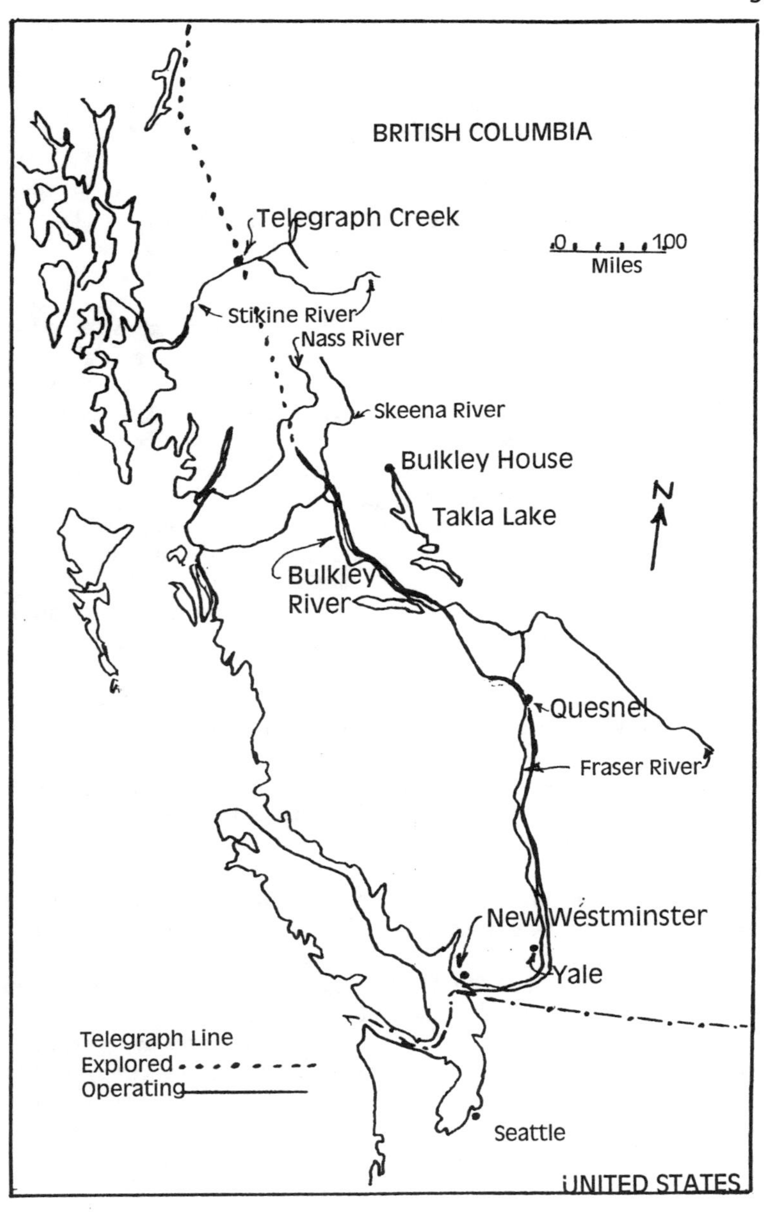
BRITISH COLUMBIA
Telegraph Creek
0 100
Miles
Stikine River
Nass River
Skeena River
Bulkley House
Takla Lake
N
Bulkley
River
Quesnel
Fraser River
New Westminster
Yale
Telegraph Line
Explored
Operating
Seattle
UNITED STATES

between them and the post office.

At Christmas the ten men at Bulkley House invited natives in for shooting matches and snowshoe races. A woman's race over five hundred yards of unbroken snow highlighted the celebration. Betting favorites were a 12-year old, a 20-year-old, and an 85-year old. The 20-year-old won, and received a red handkerchief for her prize. Between their larder and their hunting bag, the telegraph builders had a dinner of grouse pie, roast beaver, apple and bread sauce, plum pudding, and cheese and mince pies. A native brought a small keg of rum, and the dance that followed was noisy and energetic.

Meanwhile, in summer 1865, exploration continued in the other divisions of the proposed line. They planned to cross Bering Strait (178 miles) and Anadyr Bay (209 miles) and then continue two thousand miles to the mouth of the Amur. Major Serge Abasa, a Russian nobleman, commanded the three men assigned to locate the proposed route in Siberia

One of those men was George Kennan, who had been turned down for Civil War service because of physical weakness. A young telegraph operator in his father's telegraph line in Ohio, Kennan had invested his savings in the Western Union Company and applied for the expedition. His service led to a lifetime infatuation with Russia.

The Siberian crew sailed to Petropavlosk on the Kamchatkan peninsula. The town's three hundred residents had not received mail from the outside world for over three years, and Major Abasa doubted that the promised cooperation of his country in the venture would ever amount to anything. Nevertheless, they established headquarters at Gizhiga on the protected coast of the Okhotsk Sea, bought cold weather fur clothing, learned to ride reindeer, and began looking around. The cockroaches were so bad, they left their doors open at night to kill them.

The Russian-America section sailed to Sitka, headquarters for the 21 North American fur-trading stations of the Russian-American Company. The eight hundred residents of the town gave them a hearty welcome and introduced them to the custom of "15 drops." This was a half tumbler of anything from good cognac to fiery vodka, to be tossed down in a single gulp. They sailed through the Aleutians to St. Michael and a redoubt on Norton Sound, which would be the base for exploration.

Unlike the American workers in the telegraph company, the Russian employees of the redoubt were convicts serving prison sentences by exile to America. The crew had time to look around, but cold weather precluded much exploration. When the temperature dropped to sixteen degrees below zero, one member wrote in his diary that he "would not wonder if cool weather could set in soon."

The British Columbia crew eventually explored to the Stikine. There they built a boat from the remains of old miner's sluice boxes left in the 1862 gold rush, and they floated to the river's mouth. The construction crew crossed the Skeena and built the line to a point in the headwaters of the Nass River. That's as far as the operating line was ever built. The village on the Stikine which the exploring crew reached is still called Telegraph Creek.

In summer, 1865, seven years after his last attempt, Cyrus Field tried again to lay a telegraph cable on the floor of the North Atlantic. The British government had appointed a commission to study whether submarine cables could ever work, since a cable laid across the Red Sea had suddenly gone silent, as had Field's earlier cable.   But Field, encouraged that cables had crossed the Persian Gulf and the Mediterranean Sea, tried again.

In 1858, no ship could carry more than half the cable needed for the crossing, and the problem encountered then appeared to be in the splicing of the cables. But now the *Great Eastern* had been launched. She was large enough for six thousand passengers, and the three companies that had owned her had gone bankrupt because they could never fill the ship.

The current owner of the ship refused to sell to Western Union, but he was willing to make a bet. If the cable company succeeded in laying the cable with his ship, he wanted a quarter million dollars in stock; if they failed, they would owe nothing. The company took the bet, and it successfully laid the cable in July, 1866. The ship owner became a major stockholder in Western Union.

In March, 1867, Western Union advised William Seward, by then Secretary of State, that since the Atlantic had now been crossed, it was abandoning the project to cross the Pacific.

Three weeks after the company's announcement, the United States Government bought Russian America—from then on called Alaska—for seven million dollars. Some thought British Columbia, now bordered on two sides by the United States, would follow. But it joined the Dominion of Canada, which was also created that year of 1867.

Collins, his dream abandoned, returned to his earlier proposal to move ice from Alaska to become drinking water in American cities. So far, however, the acquisition of Alaska is the main benefit we have received from the failed attempt to reach Asia by telegraph.

Suggested reading: Rosemary Neering, *Continental Dash* (Ganges, B. C.: Horsdal & Schubart, 1989).

THE MAN WITH A THOUSAND PARTNERS

James Cash Penney Jr. grew up frugal, dependable, and honest. Penney, Sr., a Missouri minister, taught his son to work hard and live by the Golden Rule. Young Jim learned well. By the age of eight, he was earning all the money needed to buy his clothing.

Jim was eighteen when his father died. Two years later, he moved west to a drier climate.

In April, 1902, Jim Penney opened the Golden Rule store in Kemmerer, a mining town in southwestern Wyoming. He borrowed fifteen hundred dollars to buy a one-third interest in the business, and he became the manager.

The one-room store had a single window. Jim and his wife and their one-year-old baby lived in the attic above. They carried their water from a Chinese restaurant up the street. Jim made counters and shelves from the boxes and crates that brought him his first stock of merchandise. He carried three boxes up the outside stairway to the living quarters above. A dry goods box became their table; two shoe boxes, their chairs.

Right at the start Jim Penney established two firm rules for the store. First, it would be cash and carry — no credit, no delivery charges. He sold at the lowest possible prices. Customers paid only for the merchandise they could see. No charges were hidden.

From this came the second rule. Merchandise would never be discounted to increase sales. Sales would be used only to eliminate outdated inventory no longer handled.

Jim's banker said it would never work. Kemmerer was a company town. The five hundred coal miners who lived there shopped at the company store. Their cash disappeared soon after payday. But Jim mailed each of the miners a letter, inviting their business and listing his prices.

Jim opened at sunrise on opening day. The last customer left at midnight. Jim and his wife sat on their shoe box chairs in their small attic quarters and counted pennies, nickels, dimes, and an occasional dollar bill. They had taken in $466.59.

"I wonder what they'll think at the bank to see all that cash money," Jim said, as he blew out the kerosene lamp and went to bed.

"They'll be impressed with you Jim," his loving wife replied.

"It was both of us."

From then on, Jim did not open until seven each morning, but the store was open seven days a week. Closing time depended on the circumstances. If Jim could not see any people in the street, whether on foot or horseback, and if the hour was reasonable for such inactivity—such as ten o'clock—he would close up.

For Penney, a merchant's greatest sin was to let a customer out without buying anything. One day a railroad worker came in to buy light weight, woolen underwear. Jim showed what he had.

"It's all too heavy," the man said.

Penney, polite but persistent, led the man to a different counter.

"This is just the weight you want," he said. "Of course, it's women's underwear, but who will know beside yourself?"

Twenty minutes later Penney closed the sale. Twenty years later, the railroad man saw him in another town.

The former customer grinned, held out his hand to introduce himself, and said, "I've always wanted to see you again, Mr. Penney. When I got home the day I bought the ladies' underwear and thought about what I'd done, I put it in my trunk to remind me that a man will buy anything if the salesman is good enough."

Jim smiled and nodded pleasantly. Then the railroad man continued.

"A few years later, I got married. It took me longer to explain that underwear to my bride than it did for you to sell it to me."

At the end of the first year, Jim had taken in twenty-nine thousand dollars, and he paid off the bank loan. Four years later, when he was managing two more stores, he bought his partners out.

Jim dreamed of a chain of stores throughout the Rocky Mountains. Each would be managed by a man who fit Jim's pattern. He watched his clerks carefully to find such persons.

If Jim dusted the shelves inside or swept the walk outside and found no dirt, he asked which clerk had done the cleaning. Then he watched to see if the behavior was a habit. He let selected clerks buy in as partners and manage their stores. Above all, they had to be loyal to what Jim called the integrity of the business. By this he meant that the merchandise had to be the best possible value and sold for less than the competition.

Jim did not worry about style. Customers in small western towns did not read fashion magazines. When the J. C. Penney Company became the largest department store in the world, its founder was affectionately called the man with a thousand partners.

Suggested reading: Norman Beasley, *Main Street Merchant* (New York: Whittlesey House, 1948).

ORDERING INFORMATION

Our True Tales of the Old West
are projected for 38 volumes.

For Titles in Print,
Ask at your bookstore
or write:

PIONEER PRESS
P. O. Box 216
Carson City, NV 89702-0216
(775) 888-9867
FAX (775) 888-0908

Other titles in progress include:

Californios
Western Duelists
Frontier Lumbermen
Old West Artists

Frontier Militiamen
Ghosts & Mysteries of the Old West
Visitors in the Old West
Scientists & Engineers on the Frontier